Frank Cappiello's New Guide To Finding The Next Superstock

Frank Cappiello

LIBERTY HOUSE®

LIBERTY HOUSE books are published by LIBERTY HOUSE, a division of TAB BOOKS Inc. Its trademark, consisting of the words "LIBERTY HOUSE" and the portrayal of Benjamin Franklin, is registered in the United States Patent and Copy-right Office.

FIRST EDITION
FIRST PRINTING

Copyright © 1988 by Frank Cappiello
Printed in the United States of America

Library of Congress Cataloging in Publication Data

Cappiello, Frank A.
[New guide to finding the next superstock]
Frank Cappiello's new guide to finding the next superstock / by
Frank Cappiello.
p.   cm.
Bibliography: p.
Includes index.
ISBN 0-8306-3041-4
1. Investments. 2. Stocks. 3. Speculation. I. Title.
II. Title: New guide to finding the next superstock.
HG4527.C293   1988
332.63'22—dc19   88-25033
                                                                CIP

TAB BOOKS Inc. offers software for
sale. For information and a catalog,
please contact TAB Software Department,
Blue Ridge Summit, PA 17294-0850.

Questions regarding the content of this book
should be addressed to:

Reader Inquiry Branch
TAB BOOKS Inc.
Blue Ridge Summit, PA 17294-0214

Cover photograph by Ellen Jaffe.

Contents

To my friend and colleague—

Of the dozens of panelists who have appeared with me on "Wall $treet Week" since it began in 1970, none has been invited more often or provided more enjoyment and profitable advice than Frank Cappiello.

Those who have kept a long-term score, as I have, know that Frank is one of America's most brilliant securities analysts and guides to investment profitability.

I am delighted (as, indeed, we all should be) that my friend and colleague has now set down, in this book, his own methods for finding "super stocks." He has few peers as a super stockpicker. And, in the better environment for economic growth and equity investing that all rational Americans devoutly hope to see in this decade, we can surely use all the help we can get. Thanks, Frank, for again being there when we needed you, with the substance and the smile.

Louis Rukeyser

Foreword

Like everybody else, investors make all kinds—and lots of—mistakes. If they didn't, they'd all own the proverbial yachts. During my fifty years of investments counseling, I've looked at thousands of investors' portfolios and have seen at first hand both their successes and their failures.

One of their most common errors is the failure to keep investments in tune with the times—to prune out the dead wood in sick and dying industries—and to put some money into the rapidly growing, successful companies that can offset the inevitable future havoc wreaked by politicians, regulators, and tax collectors.

Everybody dreams of finding another IBM or Xerox or Hewlett Packard—one of the "Super Stocks," as this volume classifies them. Only a few thousand dollars put into any of these companies as they were rolling down the runway catapulted their lucky owners into the top tax brackets.

And as our author points out, the *best* time to search for potential Super Stocks is in a period of lackluster economic activity when uncertainty and gloom are the passwords. In other words, in times such as the present.

The author gives much useful, practical information and advice on how to identify a future wonder stock. He lists the characteristics which all of yesterday's big Super Stocks had in common, he illustrates his selection process with specific examples, and he concludes that tomorrow's big winners will embody most, or all, of these same qualities. This is a helpful, thoughtful volume for investors who are serious about achieving superior investment results.

Out of the thousands upon thousands of stocks available for

investment today only a tiny fraction of 1 percent will turn out to be the actual Super Stocks of tomorrow. Moreover, by the very nature of the hazards inherent in companies with extraordinary growth rates, those companies that now fully measure up to our author's stringent standards can be blown away even before their own managements know what's happening.

Given this background, my caveat to readers is: Don't settle on one or two issues as the potential key to your investment Shangri-La. Pick—by the author's qualifications—a dozen or so and hope you'll be smart enough (or lucky enough) to have chosen at least one of what future investment historians will be calling the IBM of the 1990s.

DAVID BABSON

Preface to the
Revised Edition

It was the best of times, it was the worst of times, it was the age of wisdom, it was the age of foolishness . . . it was the spring of hope, it was the winter of despair, we had everything before us, we had nothing before us, we were all going direct to Heaven, we were all going direct the other way.

From *A Tale of Two Cities*
by CHARLES DICKENS (1859)

The above passage could have been written yesterday, today, or even for tomorrow. At any point in time, there will be some "experts" eager to tell you that we are in the midst of the biggest boom in the history of Wall Street while other "experts" proclaim the current period as Wall Street's biggest bust. There is always a veritable glut of information, theories, and advice circulating about the course of the stock market, particularly during periods of high anxiety such as a bear market.

In 1981 when I began work on this book, the literature on "growth" stock investing was sparse. This scarcity was not due to lack of material since there had been a deluge of articles and scholarly monographs on the difficult stock market period of the 1970s. There was, however, the damage and residue of the "crash" of the 1973–1974 bear market still lingering in the minds of investors, both individual and institutional, from Main Street to Wall Street. Article after article in the financial news focused on the inability of most money managers to better the market averages—particularly the S&P 500 on an annual basis. Most of these articles and commentaries were by enthusiastic amateurs or financial journalists, fascinated by the apparent failures of the professionals to profit from Wall Street. Some serious researchers (mostly academicians) collected reams of material designed to prove that the market was truly "efficient," that is, in the long run, no one can do better than average.

What is the efficient market theory? It starts with a definition: a perfectly efficient market is one where the price of every security equals its investment value at all times. (For the financially literate, that means the market price of stock equals the present value of its future prospects.) This perfection is achieved when all investors have access to all currently available information about the future. It assumes that all participants are good analysts, follow market prices, and adjust their stock positions accordingly. In short, a perfectly efficient market is one where an amazing amount of information is fully and immediately reflected in prices.

Great theory, but you know the average person wouldn't recognize a piece of information if it ran into his or her car. But not to worry: the theory takes this difficulty of recognition into account beautifully by stating that EMT has three "forms."

The *strong form* argues that all current information, public and private, is reflected in stock prices; the *semistrong form* says that only publicly available info is; and the *weak form* restricts what is known to the basic trade-off between return and risk reflected in prices of securities.

While many of these researchers did provide valuable statistical insights for stock market history, a number of researchers were engaged in primarily grinding their respective axes.

Wall Street did not embrace the efficient market completely but it did lead, by the late 1970s and early 1980s, to a wave of indexing, that is, setting up a money pool to invest in the S&P 500—the market itself. The concept was that if you can't beat them, join them! Put another way: if you have difficulty achieving average market performance, then invest in the market itself by pouring all your management funds into an index fund (usually one that mirrors the S&P 500).

Ironically, just as the switch to "indexing" became a torrent, the great bull market that began in August of 1982 made investment managers (particularly those that operate stock mutual funds) successful and increasingly popular. By the early summer of 1984, there were few doubters left as to the virtue of "stockpicking," particularly focused on growth stocks. It was at that point that the market embarked on a truly remarkable advance, taking the Dow Jones Industrial Average from a low of 1086.57 (July 24, 1984) to a record high of 2510.04 in 753 trading days.

The unprecedented characteristic of this 130 percent plus advance was that the Dow doubled in price without suffering at least a 10 percent correction during this period. Growth stocks investing was "in," particularly those stocks with "super" growth.

In late August of 1987 as the Dow crossed the 2700 mark, stock prices topped out (at 2722.42) and began to sag under the deadly weight of rising interest rates and an alarmingly large trade deficit. By October 13th, the Dow had moved down in a seesaw pattern to 2508. From that point on, the stock market fell like a stone, day after day, in a panic plunge of proportions not seen since another October a long time ago, in 1929. At the market close on October 19th, the Dow had plunged to a low of 1738.74; more than 500 of those points were lost in one day (October 19th).

The decline of over 36 percent from the market's all-time high in August vaporized the stunning advances of the intervening months along with many investors' paper profits. A year-end rebound in stock prices soothed the nerves of many market watchers and heartened some investors. Amazingly, measured annually, the Dow Jones Industrial Average ended the year 1987 at 2 percent above where it started 12 months earlier!

But no one will remember 1987 as a positive year for stocks. Further, the year 1988 has proven to be a confusing one: market up, market down, fear of recession to be replaced a few months later by fears of inflation. But one thing has become obvious in the minds of the experts and pundits on Wall Street: stock investing for capital appreciation is out. It's too dangerous to your wealth! Conservative, solid investing is in.

Since the passage of the Tax Reform Act of 1986, the most talked-about change for investors has been the removal of preferential tax rates on capital gains. Capital gains are now taxed at the same rates as dividends and interest. This has led most observers to ask: Since current income is worth as much as capital appreciation, why should investors take the risk?

The answer is simple: Growth is worth more because growth in a company's value is not taxed until the investor sells the stock. In contrast, a portion of every dividend check is taken away in taxes. Put another way, as long as you hold a growth stock, you can keep 100 cents of every dollar of market appreciation and that money keeps working for you on a compounding basis. Compare this to earning dividends of which you get to keep—and reinvest—only $.67 to $.72 out of each dollar of income depending on your tax bracket.

Now, the market has once again come full circle. Nothing really has changed from the day I came into the investing business in the bear market of 1962 (when "growth" investing was suddenly a bad word), through the euphoric years of 1963 to 1966, to the crunching bear market of 1973 to 1974. The one constant then was: buying for growth was out of fashion . . . until the next time! Well, this is the next time and the search for the next Genentech, Microsoft, Compacq Computer, or a Marriott and McDonald's goes on and will always be highly rewarding.

This new edition is an attempt to reaffirm the most successful investment style in financial history: growth stock investing. Properly executed, the approach will never fail to reward you well. It updates the approach consistent with changes that have occurred in the 1980s, with the addition of some helpful tools techniques that are outlined in the greatly enlarged Appendices.

Despite what all these "experts" might say, surviving a bear or down market doesn't require a complex strategy. It simply requires that you use basic common sense and stay ahead of what's going on in the economy and the stock market. For this reason, I have included two new chapters in this edition: Bear Market Investing (Surviving Down Markets) and The Chicken Investor (Handling Price Risks).

Many people freely made available the fruits of their own labors in investment research and security analysis including Elizabeth Dater of Warburg, Pincus Counsellors, Inc.; John M. Templeton of the Templeton Funds; and Monte J. Gordon, Director of Research at the Dreyfus Funds. Monte was particularly helpful in tracing several "super stock" success stories. Additionally, Perry H. Bradlee, head of David L. Babson & Company, Inc. placed the results of some of his research at my disposal. To all of them I owe a deep debt of gratitude. The responsibility for what I have made of their material is mine, and I hope they are content with the end product.

Several debts are even greater: to Joyce Stewart, I am grateful for her thoughtful editing and incisive suggestions. And I owe a special debt to two members of my staff: Patricia Smith, diligent and faithful, who labored long and hard at the word processor; and the ever-constant Sharon Silvestri, who did the same. Both worked long hours against deadlines, and for that I can only say: thanks.

I owe the greatest debt of all to a most remarkable person: my wife, Marie. She has kept the proverbial home fires burning and waged constant warfare against bad writing, which I resisted only to my own disadvantage. Finally, to Frank Rhodes, Annmarie and Elaine Rahily (my son and daughters), who endless times during weekends honored the depressing excuse: "Your father is working."

FRANK CAPPIELLO
Baltimore
1988

Credits

All stock charts appearing in Chapters 1 through 4 are reprinted courtesy of:

M.C. Horsey & Company, Inc.
120 South Blvd. Box H
Salisbury, Maryland 21801

The publisher thanks the following corporations and individuals for the use of their photographs and assistance:

Introduction

About 5 years ago, on a flight to Seattle, I was questioned by a fellow passenger on how to make money on Wall Street. "If I could get the kind of inside information that you people get," she said, "I'd make a fortune!"

She, like so many people, views successful investing as simply profiting from tips, rumors, and trading. It's true, anyone can make a quick trading profit once in a while, and some do it frequently. But making *big* money in the stock market is not quite that easy. Real success on Wall Street requires planning, dedication, and hard work, as with any other business. It is easy to be charmed by stories of people like the taxicab driver in Rochester, New York, who, based on the advice of one of his passengers, put his modest life savings into Xerox stock in 1958 and emerged a millionaire a few years later. That was pure luck, of course.

Finding super stocks—shares that multiply many times over for sound, fundamental reasons—is not an impossible task. It can be done . . . it has been done . . . and it will be done time and time again in the years ahead.

Every successful investment practitioner I've ever met has a philosophy and a method, along with a battle plan to make it all work. And each approach is carried through with discipline and dedication. However, nearly all require a combination of sophisticated financial, accounting, and technical knowledge—*and* a constant flow of timely information leading to the right decisions.

The one method that can work for all investors, professionals on Wall Street or "the little guy" on Main Street, is outlined in detail in this book. This approach has succeeded for countless investors. It is not a secret. In fact, its tenets are known by many experienced Wall Streeters. But it is not widely used because it requires dedication, hard work and, most of all, patience. The method stresses fundamentals, as does consistent success at just about anything. Years of trial and error have been distilled into a scorecard. The answers found on these sheets will be the result of your research and analysis. The scorecard will guide you, provide some discipline, and hopefully keep you on track in your search for the next super stock.

This is a "how-to" book for the serious investor. Read it carefully, collect and study company material, refer back to the text, and use the scorecard. Once you get into it, you'll find that research can actually be exciting and fun. And, in the end, finding a super stock will be not only intellectually satisfying, but financially rewarding. I cannot promise that this book will make you rich. But it might.

1
The Outlook:
Never Brighter!

HOW CAN ANYONE BUY STOCKS WITH *ANY* DEGREE OF CONFIDENCE TO-
day? The problems seem insurmountable. Will we never be free of
this vicious cycle between inflation and recession? Clearly, the Federal
Budget Deficit is still too high and interest rates are completely unpredictable. And what of the uncertainty in the Middle East? That cannot
be ignored. How can *anyone* be optimistic, let alone make money in
the stock market with such an environment?

THE RIGHT TIME TO INVEST

People have a tendency to see the dangers and problems of the
present as being peculiar in what historians call ''chronocentrism.''
The feeling that the past was superior in terms of living quality, safety,
and investment opportunity is not unique to our time. Every generation
in history has felt that the past was better—including our own childhood.
We forget our personal fears, the anxieties of adolescence and the
uncertainty of early maturity. Indeed, any close review of historical
periods that seemed to represent idyllic conditions would reveal
anxieties and calamities.

Consider the England of Robin Hood and Friar Tuck or of Richard the Lion-Hearted. This was a period of clear heroes, well-defined villains, and a happy peasantry feasting on venison and wine. Hardly! Robin Hood's England was one of banditry, starvation, and capricious rule by a too-often absent king. Others yearn for the age of faith—of monasteries and St. Francis of Assisi. Actually, the age of Faith was an age of filth—a lack of sanitation, poor diets, even poorer medical care, and an early death by most. For Americans, the most tranquil period of our history appears to most to be the early 1900s in the Middle West. We recall the wide vistas of Kansas wheat fields, the large families and mother canning the fruit of the family labors—the Land of Oz, Dorothy and the Wizard. A nice fable, but hardly true. Dorothy of Oz would have been worked to death or boredom in the Kansas of the 1900s. The family worked from dawn to dusk. They ate well in the summer, if they were lucky, but usually went hungry in the winter. Furthermore, chances were high that one of the children would die of diptheria, or tuberculosis, or due to a simple operation in a "hospital."

The fact is, today's problems are not new problems. Concerns of inflation, recession, interest rates, and international conflict have threatened investors in one way or another, and in varying degrees, since the end of World War II. A few hours reading old newspapers in the local library will quickly lay fears to rest.

But, is it not true that enormous sums of money have been lost in the stock market over the past 20 years? After all, haven't the bear markets of 1961-62, 1973-74, 1981-82 taught us anything? Surely, there are better investments than stocks!

Indeed, most observers think that stocks in particular and the stock market in general have been poor places to invest over the past two decades. Using the Dow Jones Industrial Average as an example, they note that the Dow average of 30 stocks hit 1,000 in 1966, crossed 2,000 in early 1987 and 2700 plus in August of that year, only to plunge below 1800 in just a few months! Take your marbles elsewhere, they say, there are better games in town.

Actually, these financial pundits have overlooked, forgotten, or never knew that there are stocks and then there are *super stocks;* there is a stock market and then there is a *super* stock market. And they barely know each other.

The Dow is only one of several averages; yet, it is the most widely used indicator of stock prices because its history goes back to the end of the last century. As a result, the Dow (including the transportation and utility indices) has an attractive historical base of data for financial reporters and market observers. But the Dow as a reflector of the overall stock market can be misleading because of its nature and large company bias. It obscures the opportunities being realized every year from the more rapidly growing segments of our economy. Further, from time to time, companies are added or deleted, which create erratic patterns in the Dow. One of the often-quoted cases in point is IBM. In 1939, IBM was removed from the Dow 30 and AT&T was substituted. Ironically, if IBM had stayed in the Dow, the average would have reached a December high of 1017.39 in 1961! Instead, the Dow was at 734.91 (To add further to the irony, it is worth noting that IBM has since been reinstated as a member of this elite group.)

Other stock market averages have done better than the Dow in the past, including the next most quoted index: the Standard & Poor's Stock Price Index of 400 industrial stocks; and, like the Dow, the S&P also has financial, transportation, and utility indices. The Common Stock Index, a composite of all equity issues listed on the Exchange, has also appreciated more than the Dow in most recent years. Finally, there are the indices of the smaller companies such as the over-the-counter National Quotation Bureau Industrial Average index and the Value Line composite of 1600 stocks that have both reached new highs while the Dow struggled to regain its former record level. Unlike the Dow, these indices more closely reflect the experience of the past decade, demonstrating that the stocks of small- to medium-size companies have done substantially better than larger companies.

Some experts still point out, by using all traditional measures, that stocks cannot compare with investment returns from nonfinancial assets such as antiques, gems, Chinese ceramics, and, of course, real estate. And, while this is perfectly true, the experts are again comparing apples and oranges. No, in recent years, most stocks can't hold a candle to certain nonfinancial assets, but super stocks are another story altogether. They can easily match the return on Chippendale chairs or Persian rugs and frequently do better.

Regardless of the time period selected, super stock examples are everywhere. In 1952, a year riddled with the uncertainties of the Ko-

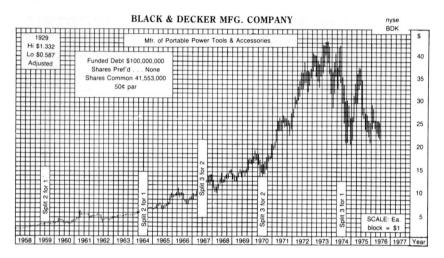

BLACK & DECKER MFG. COMPANY

rean War, controls, and concern about the course of the postwar economy, the shares in a small tool company called Black & Decker were available for $35. The company had just declared a 3 percent stock dividend, the first in a long series of stock dividends and splits. By ignoring the problems of the day and analyzing the company's past and potential performance, Black & Decker would have been recognized as a super stock. One hundred shares purchased for $3,500 would have grown to 2,350 shares by late 1973, worth an astounding $286,112 without a single additional dollar of investment in those 21 years. The steadily increasing dividends during that time would have provided thousands of dollars of income.

Between 1968 and 1977, Tropicana Products became a super stock by following a logical idea—squeeze oranges in Florida for Northern breakfast tables rather than pack and ship them with the attendant risk of spoilage. Tropicana backed this idea with an aggressive marketing organization, and in 10 years, expanded its sales from almost $61 million to $246 million. During the same period, earnings per share rose from 22 cents to $2.39. In 1978, the company was acquired by Beatrice Foods (and recently sold to Seagrams). An investor could have purchased Tropicana in 1968 at $4¼ and, adjusted for the Beatrice offer, the profit in 1978 would have been over 1,000 percent.

In early 1969, the shares of a small specialty chemical producer, National Chemsearch, were listed on the New York Stock Exchange for the first time. Only 2 years prior, the stock had been quoted over-the-counter at $46, with 1968 earnings projected to be $3.20 per share on sales of nearly $50 million. At the lowest point in the 1974 bear market, NCH stock had suffered a decline of 50 percent from its high 12 months earlier. Yet, 1968 investors should not have been too concerned. The stock's 1974 low was equivalent to $208 per share, before adjusting for three splits in the meantime. Moreover, by this point in time, the company's sales and earnings were nearly quadruple the levels of 1968. The all-important question then became: Could this growth continue?

In late 1971, Baker Oil Tools, founded nearly 60 years earlier, was enjoying the bounty of success. At $40 per share, its stock, listed on the New York Exchange, had risen 300 percent from its lows of 3 years before. For the first time in the company's history, annual sales would reach $100 million, and earnings were expected to exceed $1.80 per share! Indeed, prospects seemed bright since this company's products would be used by others wanting to "stimulate" the production of older oil wells. Nine years later, in 1980, Baker's sales rose above $1.5 billion, earnings reached the equivalent of nearly $17 per share on the original stock, and the price of each share, before adjustments for splits, topped the equivalent of $424, a gain of nearly ten-fold.

Of course, today's observer only sees the Tropicanas, the Bakers, and the Black & Deckers in retrospect, after the fact. And even though they are exceptional winners, they are not rarities. In every economic period, whether interest rates are rising or falling, whether the economy ascends or descends, or whether the "cold war" once again heats up, there are winning super stocks. And super stocks will do well even if they are bought at their highs.

Take the year 1966 for example—a time when the inflation rate first began to move up, a war in Vietnam widened, and "Great Society" programs emerged to push inflation even higher. In such an environment, what could be better than the safest of all blue chips, American Telephone & Telegraph? Had AT&T been purchased at its high that year, the results would have been less than satisfactory, however. The high in 1966 was $63. Ten years later, that same stock was again selling for $63. But more "risky" (was it, really?) was Masco, the manufacturer of a basic plumbing item: the Delta faucet. Masco, at the 1966 high, adjusted for splits, was 3 ¾. In 1976, the stock was 31 ¾! However, this stock performance did not occur in a vacuum. During this same 10 year period, sales rose from $31 million to more

The Masco "Delta" kitchen faucet.

than $400 million and earnings per share advanced from 24 cents to $1.80.

By being careful and disciplined about a stock's selection, timing in its purchase will not be a significant factor in the long run. Put another way, the right stock bought at the right time means fantastic price performance. The right stock bought at the wrong time results in substantial price appreciation over time. However, the wrong stock in the wrong market is, and will always be, a disaster!

The best time to invest is right now! Will the "market" be lower a few months from now? Maybe. But this period, and today's prices, will look pretty good to investors 5 or 10 years from now when they look back fondly and say: "Those were the good old days!"

UNLIMITED OPPORTUNITIES

Most Wall Street observers know or have heard the names Joe Wilson (Haloid Xerox), Edwin Land (Polaroid), and William McKnight (3M). These were key executives of what became major corporations during the postwar era. In recent years names like Kenneth Olson, Founder and President of Digital Equipment, and Steven Jobs, cofounder of Apple Computer, have become business and industry legends in their time. The "movers and shakers," as they are sometimes called, are often in the business news once their

*Anthony T. Rossi, founder of
Tropicana Products, now part of
Seagrams.*

The Tropicana Train for faster service to customers.

Baker International enjoyed substantial growth during the 1970's. The company's products were in great demand and management made a number of logical, strategic acquisitions. Pictured left is the Reed Rock Bit, one of the leading products of its kind in the field. Reed Tool Company was acquired in 1975. Below is Baker's Model R-3 Casing Packer which is used to control pressure and seal off a well's producing zones.

Much of Baker International's success is due to the leadership of E.H. "Hubie" Clark who joined the company as a trainee engineer in 1947 and rose to later become president in 1962. In the twenty years following Mr. Clark's appointment as president, the company's sales advanced from $30 million to more than $2 billion.

Acquisitions played an important role in Baker's progress in the 1970's. By the early 1980's, divisions acquired after 1968 accounted for about two-thirds of total sales and earnings. Two key executives responsible for the company's success in this area were James D. Woods, left, and James Joe Shelton, right.

In 1951 Black & Decker Manufacturing Company sold its one millionth ¼-inch Home Utility portable electric drill. Shown that year, from left to right, were: Robert D. Black, Honorary Chairman of the Board; Glen Tressler, Marketing Vice President; Founder Alonzo G. Decker; Inspectress Nancy Almony; Founder S. Duncan Black, and Alonzo G. Decker, Jr.

Alonzo G. Decker, Jr. joined Black & Decker in 1930, was laid off during the depression, and was later re-hired as a laborer. He worked his way up to become Chief Executive Officer in 1964. During the ten years that he held this post, B&D's sales rose from $101 million to $642 million and the company became the dominant factor in its industry.

accomplishments are better known and their companies become more important.

Indeed, investors who spend time researching young, growing businesses know this to be an ongoing, never-ending process of new names and new personalities. And yet many key people still go unnoticed. For example, each of the following men has founded a company that is today a leader in its field: Monty Rifkin, Paul Cook, and Frederick Smith—not exactly household names! Monty Rifkin is one of *the* pioneers in the cable television industry and a founder of the country's largest CATV company, American Television & Communications (now a subsidiary of Time, Inc.). Paul Cook founded Raychem Corporation, the leading producer of heat-shrinkable insulation materials for industry. Frederick Smith's report for a college economics course led to the creation of Federal Express, now a leading company in the field of overnight, small-package delivery.

What of the future? Who will be the entrepreneurs and major personalities behind the new business ventures of the late 1980s and 1990s? Only time will tell. However, it is not difficult to identify the areas that hold promise for exciting new growth companies.

A beginning assumption is that private enterprise will endure. Given the proper fiscal and monetary policies, our economic system will continue to have the power to inspire sacrifice, investment, and production. This trend will almost certainly be punctuated by recurring bouts of inflation and disinflation for brief periods, but the overall trend will be up and investors should be constantly alert for new opportunities.

Among the many promising areas in which future super stocks might be found:

Technology
- Business and office equipment
- Communications, including CATV, satellites, and video and data transmission.
- Computer software.
- Defense electronics.
- Home entertainment and home business systems.
- Materials substitution.
- Microcomputers.
- Robots.

- Specialty chemicals.
- Telecommunications.

Health and Medical

- Drugs and drug administering.
- Health care facilities and services.
- Medical devices.
- Medical equipment and supplies.

Consumer and Business Services

- Business employment services.
- Computer-related services.
- Rental services of all kinds.
- Specialty retailing.

Energy

- Conservation technologies.
- Energy alternatives, including solar and synthetic fuels.
- Extraction equipment.
- Services.
- Transportation using energy-efficient concepts.

Other

- New concepts for manufacturing and production.
- New leisure time products and activities.
- New retailing and marketing methods and services.
- Unique or specialty consumer products for the home or business.

These broad categories are not all-inclusive, of course. They are listed merely to illustrate the many possibilities. As a general rule, the new products and services in the years ahead will offer certain advantages in the marketplace. Most likely, they will be smaller or bigger, faster or slower, more efficient, more attractive, less expensive, easier to use or install, etc. Clearly, the opportunities for new growth businesses are unlimited.

CAN YOU BEAT 'EM?

During the 1970s and early 1980s, most professional money managers had great difficulty beating the market averages. This conspicuous lack of superior performance by many of the most skilled professionals on Wall Street inspired some of their clients to ask for

Texas Instruments' development of the silicon transistor in the 1950's led to a revolution in home and business electronics. Shown here is an early model of the transistor radio in 1954, both in its engineering package and as it was sold commercially.

an explanation. Since money managers have a certain fondness for steady clients, the explanation was not long in coming.

Research that had been done several decades earlier was dusted off and polished up to demonstrate that it was understandably difficult to outperform the market because the market was "efficient." That is, information about public companies is a matter of record, either at the SEC, in newspapers, at the local library, or in some other data source. The sum total of all that information and the judgments based on that information, the efficient market thesis maintained, is at all times fully reflected in the price of any given stock.

Since all security analysts have access to every shred of data, they are unlikely to uncover anything new. This felicitous discovery was followed by a second, affectionately described as the "if you can't beat 'em, join 'em" theory. If all a diligent security analyst could hope to do was match the performance of some broad market average, then why not create portfolios predesigned to duplicate the market's results? This was called "indexing" and it means to select stocks that reflect the overall composition of the Standard & Poor's 400 or 500 average.

Properly structured, the indexed portfolio would, in fact, be the "market." Not only would it guarantee satisfactory performance, but it would also reduce costs since obviously there would no longer be any need to pay analysts fancy salaries. Things were looking up on Wall Street. They were looking so good in fact that these largely defensive musings were promptly elevated to the eminence of a "theory," known in full as *Modern Portfolio Theory*. Simply stated, it is a theory of securities valuation which attempts to measure investment risk on a scientific basis.

The author of the portfolio manager's kitchen pass was Harry Markowitz, a research scientist who in the early 1950s, divided risk in common stocks into two categories: (1) market risk (known as "beta"), and (2) nonmarket risk ("alpha"). He concluded that when the market went down, some stocks performed worse than the market and that when it went up, these stocks did better than the market. A "beta quotient" was assigned to a stock. A beta of 1 assigned to a stock meant that the stock performs equal *with* the market: it would go up and down percentage-wise along with the market. A beta higher than 1 meant it is more volatile than the market and a beta of under 1 meant that it would be less volatile.

Given the power of computers to do the arithmetic and correlations and to sift through enormous amounts of data in short periods of time, it became easy to evaluate all of the better known and better-researched stocks in terms of their volatility to the market; i.e., their "betas." From this it was an easy step to develop portfolios based on "betas." If one wanted a portfolio that would be much more volatile than the market (say, do 20 percent better in an up market), it was easy enough to select stocks with betas of 1.2 or alternatively put together a package of stocks, some with betas of 1.1 and others with betas of 1.3 or 1.4, so that the average beta of the portfolio would be 1.2.

Portfolio management was relegated to simple automation

techniques, and the big investors knew the "betas" of all the big stocks. They knew everything there was to know about the IBM's, the DuPonts, and several thousands of other large companies whose stocks are heavily traded each day. As one market sage describes it: "It is as if all the institutions are Mach 3 fighter jets, armed with the latest radar to search for targets with their computer-guided missiles. There they are . . . hundreds upon hundreds of these high-capacity, electronic-powered jets stalking each other, able to assimilate mountains of data in only a few seconds. The jets are much like institutional investors, so evenly matched with their arsenals of high-powered MBA's, that they cancel out each other. When one sells IBM, they all sell IBM. When one buys Dow Chemical, they all buy Dow Chemical.

And yet, despite all this sophisticated weaponry and tracking equipment, some investors can and do make money. How come? Because at the same time the market is efficient, it is also inefficient. IBM symbolizes the efficient market. Every analyst on the street and every portfolio manager knows the data of IBM, and it's pretty hard to come up with something new. Every once in a while an analyst will put two bits of information together and get five instead of four—an inspired conclusion that will allow him and his institution to make 10 or 12 points on DuPont or Mobil Oil. But not often. The more widely owned the stock, the more "efficient" the market is in that stock; and the more likely that everything known about the stock is reflected in the price.

On the other hand, the smaller the company, the less likely that it has institutional following and the less efficient the market for its shares is likely to be. Accordingly, with smaller companies, "market inefficiencies" are the rule rather than the exception. It is here where careful analysis can yield a potential super stock.

The professional investors (those who head institutions) make up some 80 percent of the trading in the "listed stock" market. Given their billions of dollars, the emphasis is on buying stocks in companies where a sizeable investment position can be developed without running up the price. In other words, institutions want "size" in their stocks.

Recent estimates indicate that there are more than 40,000 public companies. Of these, only a fraction, a few thousand, are listed on the various exchanges—The New York and American exchanges, and so on.

Consider, too, that only another several thousand are traded with any degree of volume. The Big Five brokerage houses such as Merrill Lynch, Prudential Bache, Shearson Lehman Hutton, Dean Witter, etc., each has several dozen analysts assigned to cover several hundred stocks of interest to these institutions. For the most part, these firms each cover the same stocks. Other major research firms cover fewer, although many of these are also duplication coverage in stocks like General Motors, DuPont, etc. Essentially, all of their energies are focused on the large- or medium-sized companies. They have to be. But with all this brainpower focused on those stocks, which constitute the bulk of trading, it's hard for anyone to enjoy an advantage and to have pieces of information unknown to anyone else. Over the years, a number of academic studies have indicated that none of the major players can get an advantage and, for the most part, this is true.

However, while major studies have indicated it is hard to "beat the market" long term, there is also ample evidence that it can be done. Over the years, we in the investment business have observed that certain individuals do beat the market consistently—and when performance statistics are analyzed, it appears that they do it by investing in smaller-sized companies.

Not too long ago, *Fortune* signaled this style of investing in an article entitled: "Giant payoff from Midget Stocks" (Fortune, June 30, 1980 - A.F. Ehrbar, p. 111-114). A further study by Professor Rolf W. Banz of the University of Chicago noted that for over 54 years, smaller stocks yielded *twice* the return of stocks listed on the New York Stock Exchange.

Smaller-sized company stocks are less volatile, too. Hard to believe but true. The violent price moves in stocks in 1987 and 1988 were caused primarily by institutions making big, short-term buy-and-sell decisions. Small stocks are much less influenced by institutions. For example, within the big corporation universe of the Standard & Poor Index of 500 companies, institutional ownership declines significantly as companies get smaller—the largest 10 percent of the S & P 500 has an average institutional ownership of 47 percent, while the smallest 10 percent has an ownership percentage of only 36 percent. And for non-S & P 500 stocks, that percentage drops below 20 percent!

In point of fact, an analysis of the performance of small stocks over the past 60-odd years indicates significant periods of superior market performance, particularly after a major market decline. This was the

	Total Returns (Cumulative) After Small Stocks Underperformance					
Year Underperformance Ended	**3 Year**		**5 Year**		**10 Year**	
	Small Stocks	S&P 500	Small Stocks	S&P 500	Small Stocks	S&P 500
1931	185%	39%	559%	176%	219%	87%
1973	93	25	198	24	1,118	174

	Total Returns (Cumulative) After Major Market Declines					
Year Major Decline Ended	**3 Year**		**5 Year**		**10 Year**	
	Small Stocks	S&P 500	Small Stocks	S&P 500	Small Stocks	S&P 500
1932	323%	124%	193%	95%	386%	144%
1937	26	18	66	25	645	151
1941	319	81	542	128	1,036	393
1974	202	58	434	99	1,320	296

conclusion of a study conducted in 1988 by the David L. Babson & Co., the large mutual fund money managers. They found two periods of extended and significant underperformance by small stocks—a 6-year time span ended in 1931 and 5 years ended in 1973. The following figures show the subsequent performance of small stocks, (defined as the smallest quintile of stocks on the New York Stock Exchange), versus the S & P 500 for 3, 5, and 10 years—and the relative returns after the four declines in the S & P of over 25 percent that occurred in the past 60 years, prior to 1987s drop.

As you can see, whether following an extended period of small stock underperformance or a major general market decline, small stocks historically have rebounded powerfully. Perhaps more important, such advances have been *long lived;* investors who are concerned about the enduring performance of small stocks might find these historical precedents comforting.

At this point a skeptic would say: "But you expect to do better in smaller stocks because you're taking more risk. Higher risk equals high returns, right?" Wrong. Even adjusted for risks, smaller stocks did better.

A little thought will indicate the logic of it all. Again, the big institutions are all zeroing in on the small, but highly liquid universe of stocks they can buy. Beyond that, no one cares. There are small-sized companies in the suburbs of Tucson, Seattle, Boise, even Chicago and New York, that the institutions can't buy. And they don't care! At least for the time being. By analyzing these stocks, the average investor is not doing battle with a platoon of MBA's and a bank of computers. Later—years later—when the junior stock has grown to a sufficient size, it will suddenly be "discovered" and be entered into the thousands of computer banks of institutions and covered assiduously by analysts. At that time, the small, junior stock will soon become a super stock—fully discovered and fully-priced.

2

The Many
Roads to Success

IT IS TRUE, THERE ARE MANY ROADS TO SUCCESS. BUT ON WALL STREET,
all roads do not necessarily lead to Rome. Not every investment
approach is a reliable way to make money over the long term. Yet,
there are a few, and they will be described briefly in this chapter.

The methods vary; they can be very different, in fact. The technical
analysts track charts and indicators. The "bargain hunters" search
the marketplace for undervalued corporate earnings or assets. Many
investors look only for "turnaround situations," while "concept
chasers" are forever seeking new investment ideas that might catch
the imagination of the financial community at some point in the future.
And then, of course, there are those who swear by the growth stock
theory. (The proponents of this approach believe a stock's value will
eventually reflect the company's progress in terms of earnings,
dividends, and financial condition.)

However, investors who pursue these methods are, in their own
way, unknowingly seeking to capture profits from the inefficient segment
of the market. They are, in effect, looking for situations not yet fully

recognized by the investment community as a whole. Said somewhat differently, to quote the late Benjamin Graham: "There are two requirements for success on Wall Street. One, you have to think correctly; and secondly, you have to think independently."

Indeed, Wall Street history is replete with independent thinkers. In the 1920s and 1930s Bernard Baruch made and lost fortunes by trading on instincts and Joseph Kennedy was known in financial circles for his short selling as the stock market plunged after 1929. But they were traders with a shorter-term perspective.

By the same token, there have been many long-term investors who may also be called independent thinkers. Certainly, among them are two famous money managers, David Babson of Boston and T. Rowe Price of Baltimore. In fact, these men are credited for practically inventing the growth stock theory of investing. Both started in the 1930s, in the darkest days of the Great Depression, when no one imagined the possibility of future growth. Both have given their names to large mutual funds and investment management organizations.

Each, with his own style, emphasized taking the long-term view. David Babson, for example, would always explain his approach by saying that he wasn't "smart enough" to make money trading in the market. But he felt that the most certain way to achieve positive long-term results would be to own shares of successful companies in fields with particularly promising future prospects. This approach to investing, he maintained, would not necessarily give the *best* performance in any given period, but would surely provide better-than-average results over a long span of years. And his record certainly proved him right.

Finally, both expected to pay a premium for growth. They reasoned that if the additional cost was early enough in the game, there would be so much profit in the long run that a premium could be justified more often than not. So, in retrospect, the most profitable and lowest risk time to buy a stock of this kind was during the early stages of growth. Neither advocated "growth at any cost," but both were pioneers willing to invest for the *future*.

T. ROWE PRICE

As T. Rowe Price tells it, his investment philosophy on growth evolved back in the 1930s when President Roosevelt took the U.S. off the gold standard. At that point, Rowe Price was convinced that the country would be saddled with continuous inflation with only a few

T. Rowe Price

interruptions. He felt that investments of bonds or ordinary stocks would not be good enough to offset the lost purchasing power of the dollar. In addition, he recognized the difficulty in identifying and catching the cyclical swings of interest rates and corporate fortunes. He believed the only protection was to select stocks whose earnings were growing faster than the overall economy.

Additionally, Rowe Price has said he *expects* to pay up for an outstanding growth prospect. This, he defines, is a company whose earnings per share reaches a new high level at the peak of each succeeding major business cycle and which gives indications of reaching new high earnings at the peak of future business cycles.

Rowe Price, an authentic investment genius, has said that the individual investor can duplicate his record *if* "they select well-managed companies in fertile fields for growth and hold the stocks until it's obvious that the company is no longer growing . . . and then, and only then, is it time to sell."

Among the growth stocks in the 1930s and 1940s were chemical companies such as DuPont, Dow, and Monsanto, and Price's background was ideal for early success. As a former research chemist at DuPont, picking stocks where technology was important came as second nature. His familiarity with the dynamics of technology in chemistry was later easily transferred in the 1950s to the computer and electronics industries where the IBM's and Xeroxes were waiting to be discovered.

The selection process, according to Price, is clear-cut. His requirements for selecting "T. Rowe Price-type" growth companies have been printed and reprinted in scores of articles and printed interviews over the years. They are:

1). A fertile field (industry or business) in which to operate.
2). Superior research to develop products and markets.
3). A lack of cutthroat competition.
4). A comparative immunity from government regulation.
5). Low total labor costs, but well-paid employees.
6). The promise of a higher-than-average percent return on invested capital, sustained high profit margins, and a superior growth of earnings per share.

Armed with this list, Price notes that the successful investor must take into account the investing environment: the backdrop of social, political, as well as economic influences. The rest is simply sweat and dedication. But Rowe Price is anything but complacent or presumptuous at any given moment in time. His favorite saying, borrowed from the Greeks, but almost his trademark: "Change is the investor's only certainty."

Rowe Price's emphasis on the long-term view is based on the difficulties of successful trading. He views trading as three tough decisions: When to buy, when to sell, and, presuming one wants to keep money working long term in equities, when to buy again. Another very important reason for his long-term view: an investor who pays taxes is usually much better off by staying with a successful stock since taxes are postponed indefinitely. The trader, on the other hand, must pay taxes as well as higher brokerage commissions. The net effect is less money available for investment after each successive sell decision.

Even following his retirement from his namesake firm, T. Rowe Price Associates, Rowe Price never stopped searching for companies in expanding industries where above-average sales and earnings growth could be found. While Price seemed to favor technology where stress research, patents, and innovation, it was not always the case. Sometimes growth was found in natural resource areas, service industries, or retailing.

Once a stock was selected that fit the qualifications of growth, the question was *when* to buy—now or later. Again, Price was not averse to paying for growth, but he felt there were a few guidelines to follow:

- First, the key valuation of a stock was not asset value per share but present or future earning power per share. The record of the past would give some indication of the future. Where faster growth was projected, a higher multiple of future earnings could be paid. But he cautioned about projecting earnings growth too far in the future.

- How much you pay for earnings depends on how much can be earned on alternative low-risk investments. In other words, the yields on U.S. Treasury bills would be the minimum base on which to compare returns. Higher interest rates would mean smaller premiums for growth stocks.

- He also felt the best time to buy was when growth stocks were out of fashion.

Finally, once a stock was bought, Price left it alone in his portfolio to do its work—as long as progress continued. But nothing goes on forever and Rowe Price was quite willing to sell when earnings growth leveled out. A decline in the rate of return on stockholders' equity would be one of the most important indications.

Much can be learned by studying the accomplishments of T. Rowe Price, for he is one of the few true investment legends to come along in our lifetime.

BENJAMIN GRAHAM

The late Ben Graham, the father of modern security analysis, and also known as the "dean" of security analysts, personified the *value* or "bird-in-hand" approach to investing. His emphasis was on current dividend income, tangible asset values, and conservative valuation of earnings. He was also a college professor and a coauthor of the classic textbook *Security Analysis*. Its thesis: invest your equity money for "total return"—the sum of dividend plus potential price appreciation.

Ben Graham advocated the value, low P/E approach to investing long before it became fashionable. It was his objective to buy productive assets that could eventually produce earnings. And he wanted to buy those assets as cheaply as possible. Investors, he believed, should

Benjamin Graham

buy stocks of profitable companies at a price equal to, or less than, two-thirds of net current asset value. Above all, he sought financial soundness by avoiding companies having excessive debt. By nailing down more dividend yield now, less future price appreciation would be necessary to attain a satisfactory total return; hence, the search for below-average earnings multiples of sound stocks. In addition, there would be an extra bonus if the multiple rises along with earnings. Furthermore, if an investor can buy stock value at a significant discount, so much the better, since the stock could be a takeover candidate.

Once the stock advances 50 percent, Graham would recommend taking profits and reinvesting the money into another stock meeting the original "value" standards. Of course, unfortunately, most are of small, unknown companies.

It was Graham's opinion that the institutional investor could not, over time, obtain better results than the Dow Jones Industrial Average or the Standard & Poor's Index. "In effect," he said, "that would mean that the stock market experts could best themselves—a logical contradiction." On the other hand, he felt that the typical investor has a great advantage over the large institutions. He believed that investors willing to do a little independent research could outperform the overall market by simply stressing the value approach.

RALPH COLEMAN

Ralph Coleman, who died at a relatively young age in 1980, was a rare combination—a financial journalist and investment manager. He

Ralph P. Coleman, Sr.

was founder and president of the Over-The-Counter Securities Fund and the publisher of the *Over-the-Counter Securities Review.*

The investment approach Ralph Coleman advocated was simple and straightforward: "Buy small bargains!" Moreover, it was his opinion that, for the most part, stocks of this type would most likely be found in the over-the-counter market.

In an interview just before he died, Coleman offered a few opinions regarding the following "rules" widely used on Wall Street:

1). There is no point trying to buy "well-managed companies," since companies that are widely recognized as such are usually overpriced.
2). Gerald Loeb always used to say "Cut your losses, but let your profits run." Coleman disagreed by arguing that investors who do this will always find themselves selling good or bad stocks at the bottom.
3). It is a bad idea to be buying "what the institutions are buying." Coleman maintained that the institutions buy the "hot stocks" after most of the move has taken place.
4). Buying "big, well-established companies" is not necessarily the answer. Coleman considered companies in this category to be too large for substantial appreciation and oftentimes mature and "over-the-hill."

"My fundamental research consists basically of annual reports, quarterlies, and other published material available to everyone," he would say. He, like T. Rowe Price and Ben Graham, spent much time pouring over data of unknown companies. The inefficient market segment was, in effect, his "element."

OTHER "INDEPENDENT THINKERS"

One of the most successful investment managers on the West Coast, Claude N. Rosenberg, Jr. made his mark in the 1960s in growth stocks when he was head of research of a regional brokerage firm. He went on to found the highly successful Rosenberg Capital Management, Inc., which manages billions of institutional and pension fund dollars.

Among Claude Rosenberg's early successes were small growth companies, which he called "bikini" stocks, named after the small bathing suit. When related to growth companies, however, it meant explosive potential earning power, coupled with a small amount of stock outstanding.

Claude Rosenberg's view is that large companies with huge capitalizations must develop a constant stream of new products to fuel large earnings increases. On the other hand, a single product or service in a "bikini" company would result in an immediate and magnified effect on earnings and on the stock price. Rosenberg has always been quick to point out the reverse can also be true. A product that fails to meet expectations can have a disastrous effect on earnings—and perhaps on a company's solvency as well.

In the difficult investment environment of the 1980s with two vicious bear markets (1980 to 1982 and 1987 to 1988) and one huge and profitable bull market (1982 to 1987), a handful of successful money managers stand out above the crowd: Peter Lynch, Warren Buffet, and John Templeton.

Peter Lynch

One of the most esteemed fund managers and stockpickers is Peter Lynch, who supervises Fidelity Investments' Magellan Fund. This multibillion-dollar fund has been managed by Lynch since June of 1977. Since then, the fund has compiled one of the best long-term performance records in the business. If an individual had invested $10,000 in the Fund in 1976 just before Lynch took over, he would have had a portfolio worth more than $170,000 by the end of 1986.

Peter Lynch, supervisor of Fidelity Investments' Magellan Fund.

How does he do it? What are some of the secrets of his success? One of his "secrets" is that he works hard—typically, a 70-hour-plus work week, visiting over 200 companies every year and reading over 700 annual reports. This is in addition to keeping contacts with different people throughout the country. He is a great believer in Thomas Edison's theory of genius: it's 99 percent perspiration.

Another factor Lynch considers to be crucial to stockpicking success is: *Focusing on the quality of the company's products or services.* According to Lynch, you shouldn't buy a company's stock if you wouldn't buy its products: check the usefulness and desirability of what the company produces. Simply observing the product's grocery store shelfspace and advertising can give you an idea of how it's doing. For instance, one of Lynch's more successful investments has been in the cable video network business. His interest developed after he heard his daughter make a complimentary remark about a cable television station.

A third guideline for rewarding stockpicking is to buy whenever you see an attractive value, regardless of your feelings about the market overall. The stock should come first. Lynch also noted that if you try to predict the economy, you make mistake number one. You are better off concentrating on companies. Lynch's approach is completely focused on individual stocks, not the overall stock market, because he believes that it's very hard to predict the market's future behavior.

On holding periods for stocks, Peter's time horizon is flexible. Some stocks he's owned for more than 5 years. If a company is doing well, his view is: never sell it. Other stocks such as new issues that immediately go to big premiums, will be sold in 1 day.

His minimum objective is to capture "one-third" moves. If a stock has a quick move and he makes, in a short period, what he expected to over a year or two, he's out. According to Lynch, if you can make six 30-percent moves compounded, you can make fourfold on your money. You can't do that on one stock. And the usual tendency when the average investor has a 50-percent move in a stock is to get excited: hang on and wait for more. If the investor waits 4 years and the stock does nothing else but sit there on top of its 50-percent move, the result is an 8-percent compounded return over 4 years! Not all that great!

Finally, he doesn't like to "bottom fish," that is, buy stocks because they've fallen dramatically in price. According to him, a common mistake that investors make is to buy a stock because it's fallen by half or two-thirds of its former price. One of his favorite examples of the early 1980s was the Standard Oil of Ohio that in 1982 fell from 90 to 60. At that point, everyone was saying it was not going to go any lower. Then it went to 50 and finally through 40 and finally, down to under 30. Lynch's point was you never know how far down a stock will go, no matter what the quality.

He makes no attempt at market timing, usually staying fully invested, and is strictly a long-term investor. In a recent letter to Magellan Fund stockholders, he wrote:

> "I have no feeling for the direction of the market over the near term, or the next 3 to 12 months . . . and that has always been my position. All of the great advances and declines of the past 20 years have been surprises to me. The Fund has underperformed in bear markets. In each of the past eight declines of 10 percent to 30 percent over the past decade, Magellan had fallen more than the general market, and this pattern was true again in October's (1987) steep drop. If the market falls sharply

again, Magellan will also have a major decline. If an individual is not prepared for a stock, a stock fund, or the market to decline 25 percent to 35 percent in the future, he or she should be in a money market fund or the bank. My goal is to outperform the market over the long-term by 5 percent to 6 percent annually. I have been buying stocks of companies with high-quality operations and excellent prospects that have suffered sharp declines in price. If you believe, as I do, that America will continue to grow over time, and you plan to annually increase your commitment to stocks by allocating a portion of your investment dollars each year, periodic corrections are actually quite positive, because you purchase more shares for the same dollar amount.''

In the early days much of his success came from dividing the Fidelity Magellan Fund into two sections—one with small growth companies that he intended to hold for long periods of time and the other part that had relatively conservative stocks that would have a shorter time frame for success.

Amazingly, about 35 or 40 percent of the stocks he chooses are losers. Usually, the first sign of a loser is that it drops in price. At that point (or warning signal) Lynch rechecks with the company; if sales and earnings are still in an uptrend, he'll buy more. Otherwise, he concludes he's wrong and sells quickly. But, he will admit, sometimes not quickly enough. *When* to sell (or buy) can be made easier by understanding the company's business. If you don't understand the company business, you can't make a good investment judgment.

Another lesson to be learned from Lynch is to remain in control of your ego and emotions. You should worry, but not to the point where the problems and pressures interfere with your investments. Finally, Lynch advises investors always to be curious and to try to be conceptual. Visualize the future of a company, potential new products or services, and how the entire combination will develop and grow.

In summary, one of the world's most successful money managers is saying he is not concerned about whether we'll have a recession or not, or the near-term direction of the stock market. What he is concerned with is looking for growth companies and special situations at attractive prices. He is prepared for his holdings to go down, in which case he may buy more. In making his decisions, he is always looking ahead 5 to 10 years, not 5 to 10 months.

Warren Buffet

Another highly respected and astoundingly successful investor is Warren Buffett. When he dissolved his original investing partnership in 1969, his initial investors had multiplied their money by 30 times in the 13 years it lasted! Buffett had never had a down year, even during the severe bear markets of 1957, 1962, 1966, and 1969. That distinction is unique among modern portfolio managers.

In the 1973-74 market collapse, Buffett bought large blocks of his favorite stocks at giveaway prices that have since tripled or quadrupled. Market forecasts are of no interest to Buffett, nor for that matter is the stock market itself. He has been quoted as saying: "As far as I'm concerned, the market doesn't exist. It is there only as a reference point to see if anybody is offering to do anything foolish (greedy, undervalued situations). When we invest, we invest in businesses." Buffett is currently the best example of a long-term buyer. He buys shares of businesses in which he perceives growth at bargain prices, confident that all he has to do in order to collect his rewards is to wait patiently and ignore Wall Street's hoopla.

John M. Templeton

John M. Templeton, the most successful long-term mutual fund manager of our time, is unique both in terms of his record and the time frames he uses. He views the future in terms of years rather than months. If you had invested $1 in the Templeton Growth Fund 33 years ago, your investment would have grown to more than $80 today.

While that is an impressive record in and of itself, it is more astounding if one considers that the Templeton Growth Fund placed consistently high (among the top twenty best-performing funds) in bull markets and among an exclusive elite of the top five funds in not losing most of those gains in a bear market. So, what are Templeton's secrets?

First and foremost is his search for significant value. He looks for companies whose stock price reflects only a small fraction of their true value. In the long run, he believes that basic values are reflected in market price. He usually finds these values among stocks that are neglected or indeed shunned by most of the investment community. This means looking at out-of-favor stocks *and* industries.

Two cases in point were Ford Motor in the early 1980s and Union Carbide at about the same time. Both stocks were considered "over the hill," that is, in nongrowth industries with a loss of market share, but where the industry continues to have growth and where management was making prodigious efforts to refurbish company operations in order to become efficient. In a sense, he was looking at these companies from a different point of view than the Wall Street majority. In both Ford and Union Carbide he achieved more than 100 percent gains.

Another factor or ingredient in Templeton's success is his consideration of the effect of inflation as an element in his investments. Simply put, any company that Templeton invests in must have the capability of being able to cope with inflation. He views inflation as inevitable and some companies and industries (such as real estate) are better able to cope than others.

Beyond these broad conceptual factors are ten specific details that Templeton searches out in his investment candidates, specifically:

1). The growth rate in earnings per share, present and future.
2). The price earnings ratio.
3). The ideal "mix"—the highest possible growth rate for the lowest possible P/E.
4). Consistency in earnings growth gets additional weight as a factor. On the other hand, growth rates that are too high could be signs of trouble since they are probably unsustainable.
5). Pretax profit margins. They should be rising.
6). Book value has some relevance as a factor.
7). Be flexible. "Flexibility" to Templeton means several things. First, it means willingness to adjust your approach when it seems advisable. It also means the ability to acknowledge investment mistakes. Everyone makes mistakes, but it's the mark of a successful investor if he can recover from those mistakes and move on. It is also important to ensure that any mistake will not be fatal. That's a good reason to be heavily diversified; you contain and limit the damage.
8). The company's overall long-range plan. (Do they have one? Is it ambitious enough?)
9). Level of the company's competitors. How effective are they?
10). Company problems other than competition (as perceived by the company).

Templeton makes substantial use of secondary sources including stockbrokers and their reports, the facts in the Value Line Investment

Survey, and, of course, the daily newspapers including the Wall Street Journal and the New York Times. Note that none of these sources are beyond the scope of the average individual.

According to Templeton, some of the things a successful investor must have to succeed would include diligent work, simpleminded common sense, thrift, prayer, and patience. "We buy for long term. Our average holding period is 6 years in stocks."

And finally, what about the future? "That's easy," Templeton notes. "The next several decades may be just as profitable as the last two decades."

Among the top-performing mutual funds of the past few years is the Putnam OTC Emerging Growth Fund—a fund that invests nearly exclusively in potential super stocks. In the 5 years ending December 31, 1987, this Fund soared 175 percent in value—ranking 11th among the more than 500 funds followed by Lipper Analytical Services, Inc., a firm that tracks mutual fund performances. Matthew Weatherbie, comanager of the Fund notes that if and when the economy turns down, it makes sense to invest in small companies. During uncertain economic conditions, small companies will deliver more predictable earnings than many economically sensitive big companies, and they are much more adaptable to changing conditions.

As an illustration of this, most of the companies in the Putnam OTC Emerging Growth Fund are expected to have earnings growth rates of 25 to 30 percent over the next couple of years. And, in 1988, these companies were selling at an average of only 14.5 times estimated 1988 earnings. In effect you could buy these stocks at just about half their annual growth rate. Compare that with blue-chip stocks, which usually have P/E ratios close to those of growth stock but have a much lower expected growth rate.

Weatherbie and Richard J. Jodka, the Fund's other manager, are "bottom up" stockpickers; that is, they are more concerned with the company's prospects than those of the economy or the market. With smaller companies, introducing new products and management changes have much more of an impact. Consequently, frequent communication with management, as well as competitors, suppliers and customers, is the only way to stay on top of each situation. Weatherbie and Jodka also look for high management ownership, which helps ensure that the investor and management have similar goals and signals that management has confidence in the company's future.

The lesson to be learned from such accomplished managers as Lynch, Buffett, and Templeton is that although the stock market is unpredictable—sometimes devastatingly so—it still offers a viable means for acquiring wealth over a period of time. The key to successful investing is a long-term approach, focusing not on market direction but on the disciplined, periodic accumulation of quality growth stocks at depressed prices, undervalued secondary or special-situation stocks, and/or quality stocks on a dollar cost averaging basis. With this approach, an investor can take even market crashes—such as 1987—in stride.

Ben Rosen

Ben Rosen, a former topflight semiconductor stock analyst and the cofounder of the most successful venture capital firm, Sevin Rosen Management, financed two of the most successful new companies in financial history: Compaq Computers and Lotus Development. His firm receives a thousand proposals to invest a year and accepts only six. In his opinion, technology is the engine of fast earnings growth and, more specifically, blinding innovation. The only way a small company can succeed against the giants is to do something so innovative that they can truly compete. If they can't do that, you should be cautious about investing in their technology.

He notes that when he started his venture capital fund, their first *and* second investments went bankrupt, but their third and fourth investments were great winners.

In Rosen's view, technology has a bright future in the investment world. This would include biotechnology, "super" minicomputers (bringing the price and efficiency of super computers down to a low level), military technology, and office automation.

3
That Magic
Combination

SMALL IS DEFINITELY BEAUTIFUL WHEN IT COMES TO ACHIEVING THE kind of growth rate that will eventually produce a super stock. For example, the opening of a new market niche might not even budge the net earnings of a company with more than $500 million dollars in revenues, but that same new market could conceivably double the net earnings of a $50 million company. (And one definition of a super stock is "A company whose earnings will increase at a rate of at least 50 percent greater than the current level of long-term interest rates.")

To generate these earnings, the super stock candidate will typically pay only a small dividend to its shareholders, preferring to reinvest the bulk of each year's earnings into new product development, new plant and equipment, or to increase the market penetration of existing products. This, is turn, will increase profitability and generate greater profits, which will then be reinvested to generate still more profits. Like the ramjet engine, the faster the jet goes, the more air to be taken in and compressed, thus propelling the jet even faster through the air. And so it is for our super stock. More money will be made to invest in new plant and equipment to produce more products at a still higher profit, which will be reinvested again, and so on.

After a time, this continued compounding of earnings will eventually be recognized in the marketplace. At that point, the consistency of earnings growth becomes a highly predictable event encouraging investors to appraise the stock at significantly higher prices. For an investor holding a super stock, dramatic earnings growth coupled with an expanding P/E multiple can be a truly magic combination.

FAST GROWTH FROM A SMALLER COMPANY

The compounding effect of sales and earnings can have a *profound* impact on the long-term results of any growth investment—especially if a rapid growth rate can be maintained for an extended period of time. However, growth can also become more difficult to attain as the business gets larger. This point is dramatically illustrated by this example: A company with sales of $50 million, and facing 5 years of 30-percent annual growth, must add $55 million to its sales base in the 6th year to continue its growth rate of 30 percent! Some can do it; many others cannot.

Therefore, logic tells us, it would seem easier for a $50 million business to double in size than it would be for a $500 million one. So, in the Wall Street arena, what is a "big" or "small" company? It depends. There is no clear answer, although an investor usually considers himself closer to the "ground floor" with a $5 million enterprise than with, say, a $500 million company.

Moreover, the term "size" has a different meaning within each industry. A $100 million publishing company is quite large; a $100 million oil services company is fairly small. And, while the management of Chrysler might not agree, other problems, such as financing, might be more difficult for a $5 million company than for a firm ten, twenty, or a hundred times its size. Of course, this is not to imply that problems of financing are peculiar only to smaller companies. But creditworthiness, which frequently comes with maturity, is by far the most important factor.

Our objective is now to identify the optimum size for investment—a company with an ability to finance itself with internally-generated funds and one that has reached a certain sustainability within its own markets. A rapidly-growing company that is too small can go unnoticed by the stock market for years. On the other hand, if the business has reached such a size that a significant portion of its entire market (or an entire new market) must be added just to maintain its earlier growth rate, the company has probably already passed its super stock stage.

As we pore through our library data, what, then, is the ideal size of our super-stock-to-be? *Experience suggests that companies with sales in the range of $25 million to $500 million should be given priority in the analysis.* Does this mean that IBM, with $734 million sales in 1956, or Eastman Kodak, with $633 million in 1954, were bad selections? Of course not. Or would it have been wrong to buy Capital Cities Broadcasting in 1963 when sales were only $17 million? No! There are no hard and fast rules on Wall Street.

Generally speaking, companies in this $25 million to $500 million range have the best of all worlds. By this time, they have "made it" in their respective markets and, at the same time, they are still small enough to enjoy significant growth. But how can potential earnings growth be gauged?

In corporate finance, the compounding effect on earnings can be measured by the *earned growth rate;* the annual rate at which the stockholder's equity or capital is increased. Stockholders' capital are those corporate assets left after deducting debt and preferred liabilities. Stockholders' equity is also synonymous with "book value."

To demonstrate the effectiveness of the buildup in stockholders' equity where a company's earnings are growing rapidly and (due to a modest dividend payout) are allowed to compound, let's take a mythical company, ABC Corporation, which has the following characteristics:

- Earnings per share growing at 20 percent a year, compounded;

- A dividend on common shares that is fixed at a 20 percent payout of earnings; and

- A current book value of $10 per share.

To calculate the effect of compounding, we use the per share book value at the beginning of the year since this is what the ABC Corporation executives had with which to work. To get our *earned growth rate,* we use the earnings per share for the year ended, less the dividend paid to stockholders. What's left is plowed back into the corporation for investment. The "plowback" in earnings is then divided by the book value at the beginning of the year to give us an earned growth rate percentage.

The formula is:

$$\text{Earned Growth Rate} = \frac{\text{Annual earnings } \textit{less} \text{ annual dividends}}{\text{Book value (beginning of the year)}}$$

Using this formula we can see how ABC Corporation's book value builds up:

Year	Beginning Value	Earnings	Dividends	"Plow Back"	Earned Growth Rate	Return on Stockholders' Equity*
1	$10.00	$ 1.00	$ .20	$ .80	8.0%	10.0%
2	10.80	1.20	.24	.96	8.9	11.1
3	11.76	1.44	.29	1.15	9.8	12.2
4	12.91	1.73	.35	1.38	10.7	13.4
5	14.29	2.08	.42	1.66	11.6	14.6
6	15.95	2.50	.50	2.00	12.5	15.7
7	17.95	3.00	.60	2.40	13.4	16.7
8	20.35	3.60	.72	2.88	14.2	17.7
9	23.23	4.32	.86	3.46	14.9	18.6
10	26.69	5.18	1.04	4.14	15.5	19.4

*To be precise, it is better to calculate ROE by dividing the earnings figure by the *average* of beginning and ending book values.

Let's assume that in year one the common stock was selling at $10 a share, right on book value since ABC Corporation was little known to investors. Put another way, at $10 a share, the investor was buying $1 in earnings—a price earnings multiple of *10*. Consider that even if the stock continued to sell at *book value*, and nothing else, our equity per share would increase 167 percent in 10 years, tax free to the stockholder!

But remember, investors often disregard book value—they buy earnings. So while equity rose 167 percent, earnings moved from $1.00 to $5.18 per share in 10 years. Assuming investors paid no more than 10 times earnings, our stock price would rise from $10.00 to more than $51, an increase of more than 400 percent!

But given the demonstrated earnings record of 20 percent compounded over a 10-year period—investors would probably appraise the stock at a higher multiple since a significant element of predictability has been indicated. A 20 percent growth rate might call for a multiple of 20 times (or more in enthusiastic markets). Applying a P/E of 20 to our 10th year earnings per share of $5.18, we could see a price of $103.60! Actually, at this point, investors would probably be looking into an 11th year of 20 percent earnings increase—an expected earnings of $6.22 per share. So our ABC Corporation stock in the 10th year could be selling at 20 × $6.22 or $124.40, an increase of 1140 percent!

A company in this $25 million to $500 million range is also much more likely to achieve dramatic results from plowback because it is still at an early stage in its corporate growth cycle. Large, blue-chip companies have long since passed the furious growth of their corporate youth.

THE LIFE CYCLE

As we search for super stocks, we're asking ourselves what every football scout asks: Where is the next superstar? He searches the colleges, looking for performance statistics that will reveal the one player who can, almost overnight, "make it" in the Pros. So too, with our search. We want a young, emerging firm with the potential to make it big—to become a large, very profitable company. We want to catch the company early when the stock price does not yet fully reflect its future earnings potential.

Although life cycles vary by company and by industry, the growth curve shown on the next page reflects the largest part of corporate experience.

If this effort is successful, we could be in a position to do what many "experienced" investors only dream of doing: to buy low and sell high. The following exhibit is the actual experience of a well-known super stock several years ago.

AN EXPANDING P/E MULTIPLE

One of the most widely used (some say overused) valuation tools on Wall Street is the *Price Earnings Ratio,* also variously called the

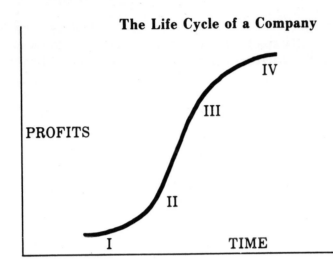

The Life Cycle of a Company

PHASE I *A NEW VENTURE!*

During the development period, the company pays little, if any, dividends to the stockholders. Most of the money invested in the company to date as been from the founders and venture capitalists. Profit margins are generally low, or perhaps non-existent at this stage.

PHASE II *THE EARLY YEARS: RAPID GROWTH*

Growth has begun and the company's profitability is becoming more evident. Profit margins are climbing and the earnings "plowback" is now financing most of the company's needs for capital. Small cash or stock dividends are declared. The company and the stock are becoming recognized!

PHASE III *CONTINUED GROWTH*

The company's profitability is now reaching its peak. Plants are being built to meet the heavy product demand. Competition is becoming more evident. Dividend increases and stock splits are almost commonplace. Now the company is a leader in its field.

PHASE IV *MATURITY*

Sharp increases in sales are becoming infrequent. At this point, either the new products developed during Phase III are starting to make a contribution or a decline is beginning to set in. Cash dividends are now a larger portion of earnings — perhaps 50% or more of annual profits. Competition is now much more intense and, while earnings may still be increasing, profit margins are declining. Analysts and brokers are currently calling the stock "a 'core holding' for long term portfolios."

"P/E ratio," the "P/E Multiple," or just simply the "P/E" or "The Multiple." By whatever name, it is a constantly varying, sometimes mysterious relationship between the stock's price and its earnings per share. Strictly speaking, the P/E is calculated by dividing the earnings per share into the stock price. Usually, the EPS figure is of the latest

The Life Cycle of One Super Stock:
A Real Life Story

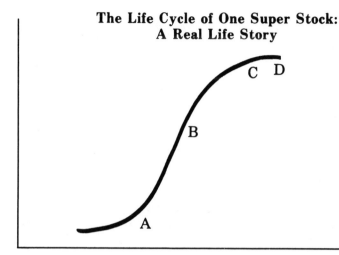

A
Year: 1
Sales: $65.3 million
Profit Margin: 24.5%
EPS: $0.23
Dividend: $0.03
Stock Price: 9 1/2
P/E Ratio: 41.3

Sales + 36% from last year; EPS + 28%; Dividends + 50%. P/E expanded from 27 to 41 times earnings; stock nearly double the price of last year.
Minor institutional interest.

B
Year: 8
Sales: $204.0 million
Profit Margin: 28.3%
EPS: $0.93
Dividend: $0.06
Stock Price: 43 3/8
P/E Ratio: 46.6

Sales + 46% from last year; EPS + 60%; Dividends + 100%. The P/E multiple is advancing and the stock is being accumulated by institutions.

C
Year: 12
Sales: $465.6 million
Profit Margin: 27.6%
EPS: $1.92
Dividend: $0.32
Stock Price: 124 1/8
P/E Ratio: 64.6

Sales + 16% from last year; EPS + 3%; Dividend unchanged from prior year; Profit margins peaked in year 11 at 31%. Institutions own the stock heavily.

D
Year: 13
Sales: $444.3 million
Profit Margin: 25.6%
EPS: $1.86
Dividend: $0.32
Stock Price: 90 7/8
P/E Ratio: 48.9

This was the first of many disappointing years. Several years later, record sales and earnings were reported, but the stock price and the P/E of this "growth stock emeritus" settled at substantially lower levels.

BRUNSWICK CORPORATION

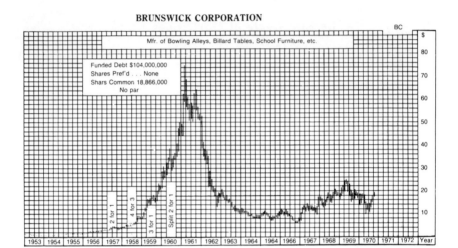

12-month period. However, it is not an uncommon practice to calculate the multiple on earnings estimated 12 months into the future (this seems especially true when stocks are rising and analysts and portfolio managers are feeling more courageous). Nor would it be an understatement to say that an entire book can be devoted to explaining the P/E multiple. The variables can boggle the mind.

The table on the next page demonstrates the important role P/E's played in five now-classic "round trips." As the figures show, when earnings are growing, an expanding P/E can result in fantastic price performance! But a rich multiple and an earnings disappointment can be as dramatic as a free-falling safe from the tenth floor.

No discussion on P/E multiples is complete without an answer to the question: "At what price?" Without becoming inextricably involved in a subject no less perplexing than the meaning of life itself, there is one valuation approach worthy of note. The table on page 44 (reproduced with permission; *Understanding Wall Street;* Liberty Publishing Company, 1982), is based on a revised version of a formula developed by the late Benjamin Graham, the "dean" of security analysts.

To use this table, the investor must first estimate the company's annual growth rate for the next 7 to 10 years. Then, by crossing this growth rate with the prevailing interest rate for Aaa bonds, the table will reveal a P/E multiple that can be used as a starting point to any analysis.

Avon Products	1955	1973	1974
Stock Price	1 3/8	140	18 5/8
EPS	0.11	2.34	1.92
P/E	12.5	59.8	9.7
% Contribution: Earnings	—	20%	21%
P/E	—	80%	79%
Brunswick Corporation	**1956**	**1961**	**1962**
Stock Price	2 1/2	74 7/8	13 1/8
EPS	0.37	2.56	1.36
P/E	6.8	29.2	9.7
%Contribution: Earnings	—	21%	57%
P/E	—	79%	43%
Fleetwood Enterprises	**1967**	**1972**	**1973**
Stock Price	2 5/8	49 1/2	3 1/2
EPS	0.18	1.21	0.44
P/E	14.6	40.9	8.0
% Contribution: Earnings	—	32%	68%
P/E	—	68%	32%
Holiday Inns	**1964**	**1972**	**1974**
Stock Price	4 1/8	55 5/8	4 1/4
EPS	0.21	1.38	1.06
P/E	19.6	40.3	4.0
% Contribution: Earnings	—	45%	25%
P/E	—	55%	75%
Polaroid Corporation	**1957**	**1969**	**1974**
Stock Price	5 3/8	145 3/4	14 1/8
EPS	0.18	1.92	0.86
P/E	29.9	75.9	16.4
% Contribution: Earnings	—	37%	61%
P/E	—	63%	39%

Price/Earnings Ratios Assuming Different Growth Rates and Interest Rates

Prevailing Interest Rate

Expected Growth Rate	3%	4%	5%	6%	7%	8%	9%	10%	11%	12%	13%	14%	15%	16%	17%	18%
20%	71.2	53.4	42.7	35.6	30.5	26.7	23.7	21.4	19.4	17.8	16.4	15.3	14.2	13.3	12.6	11.9
19%	68.2	51.2	40.9	34.1	29.2	25.6	22.7	20.5	18.6	17.1	15.7	14.6	13.6	12.8	12.0	11.4
18%	65.3	49.0	39.2	32.7	28.0	24.5	21.8	19.6	17.8	16.3	15.1	14.0	13.1	12.2	11.5	10.9
17%	62.4	46.8	37.4	31.2	26.7	23.4	20.8	18.7	17.0	15.6	14.4	13.4	12.5	11.7	11.0	10.4
16%	59.4	44.6	35.7	29.7	25.5	22.3	19.8	17.8	16.2	14.9	13.7	12.7	11.9	11.1	10.5	9.9
15%	56.5	42.4	33.9	28.3	24.2	21.2	18.8	17.0	15.4	14.1	13.0	12.1	11.3	10.6	10.0	9.4
14%	53.6	40.2	32.1	26.8	23.0	20.1	17.9	16.1	14.6	13.4	12.4	11.5	10.7	10.0	9.5	8.9
13%	50.6	38.0	30.4	25.3	21.7	19.0	16.9	15.2	13.8	12.7	11.7	10.9	10.1	9.5	8.9	8.4
12%	47.7	35.8	28.6	23.9	20.4	17.9	15.9	14.3	13.0	11.9	11.0	10.2	9.5	8.9	8.4	8.0
11%	44.8	33.6	26.9	22.4	19.2	16.8	14.9	13.4	12.2	11.2	10.3	9.6	9.0	8.4	7.9	7.5
10%	41.8	31.4	25.1	20.9	17.9	15.7	13.9	12.6	11.4	10.5	9.7	9.0	8.4	7.8	7.4	7.0
9%	38.9	29.2	23.3	19.5	16.7	14.6	13.0	11.7	10.6	9.7	9.0	8.3	7.8	7.3	6.9	6.5
8%	36.0	27.0	21.6	18.0	15.4	13.5	12.0	10.8	9.8	9.0	8.3	7.7	7.2	6.7	6.3	6.0
7%	33.0	24.8	19.8	16.5	14.2	12.4	11.0	9.9	9.0	8.3	7.6	7.1	6.6	6.2	5.8	5.5
6%	30.1	22.6	18.1	15.1	12.9	11.3	10.0	9.0	8.2	7.5	6.9	6.5	6.0	5.6	5.3	5.0
5%	27.2	20.4	16.3	13.6	11.6	10.2	9.1	8.2	7.4	6.8	6.3	5.8	5.4	5.1	4.8	4.5
4%	24.3	18.2	14.5	12.1	10.4	9.1	8.1	7.3	6.6	6.1	5.6	5.2	4.8	4.5	4.3	4.0
3%	21.3	16.0	12.8	10.7	9.1	8.0	7.1	6.4	5.8	5.3	4.9	4.6	4.3	4.0	3.8	3.6

4

Learning
from the Past

EACH YEAR THERE ARE STOCKS THAT DO BETTER THAN THE STOCK
market averages; in many cases, spectacularly better. More
importantly, there are stocks that year-in and year-out outperform the
market as a whole in good as well as bad markets. Each year we read
articles about how one investor made a million dollars buying Stock
A or Stock B or using a new failure-proof technique.

As one Wall Street expert used to say when asked about investing
success:

"Making money in the stock market is simply to have stock
you bought at lower levels go up dramatically in price and stay
there . . .

Wouldn't you have loved to have bought Scientific Atlanta at 2 or
3 during the depths of the bear market of 1974 and watched the stock
move dramatically up more than ten-fold in the next few years!
Remember Walt Disney, Xerox, McDonald's, or Houston Oil and
Minerals? And in the 1980s there were stocks like COMPAQ Computer
that went from 3½ to a high of over 60 in 1988, Lotus Development
(Personal Computer Software), and Franklin Resources (Mutual Funds

and Advisory Services). The last two stocks doubled, redoubled, and then doubled again in price in only a few years. These stocks all went up anywhere from 8 to 20 times their buying price over five and ten year periods in the past. Few of the great stock performers were new issues; and all these companies were in different industries—oil, technology, fast food. They also possessed different management styles.

Basically, the companies that made investors big money were neither very small nor very large, but something in between. The trick was to identify these companies at their "take-off" stage where the company was clearly demonstrating its ability to generate high cash profits in a growing area of activity. This is the point where you can identify a super stock and buy it cheap because most investors have not yet found it.

Year in and year out, brokers inundate investors with lists of recommended stocks. They offer stocks selling at substantial discounts from book value where ratios of recent price to tangible asset values are low (that is, they appear cheap compared to market averages); or stocks with the high dividend returns; or stocks with the lowest price earnings ratio. All these recommendations are interesting and probably of some use, but the astute investor looking for maximum appreciation will realize that:

- Discounted corporate assets are of little value unless someone else wants them at a higher price, or new management has a way to utilize those assets into producing greater earnings. After all, in the final analysis, that's what assets are for: to produce income.

- Dividends are, indeed, extremely important, as this chapter later illustrates. However, dividends are merely the *result* of earnings, secondary in importance to the plowback of earnings for continued growth. Further, dividends represent two taxes. The first is paid by the corporation; the second is later paid by the shareholder who receives the dividends.

- Low price earnings ratios (low, relative to other stocks, that is) might represent earning power at a bargain; but that's rarely the case. Usually, low price earnings ratios, particularly if they've been low for a long period of time, represent the stock market's sensing of cutthroat competition, inordinate government regulation, an industry that is declining rather than growing, and so on.

What *does* work if these methods don't? Most of the answer lies in the past. Which stocks have done well over long periods of time and why? The same stocks and the same industries rarely repeat. But the companies behind the super stocks hold some lessons that can be useful in the future. To this end, a list was compiled of many high performing stocks, in terms of capital appreciation, over the past few decades. The review included stocks of all kinds, listed or over-the-counter. The only qualification was that they be readily available for purchase by an investor.

By reviewing the winners of past decades, it was possible to identify those common characteristics these achievers seem to possess, and then to analyze and test those characteristics to the point where they could be used in sifting through thousands of stocks to identify future "super stocks."

The universe of common stocks was screened to select those that performed best in recent history. Performance meant maximum capital gains during the period studied. Once these stocks were identified, a review of their operating history was undertaken to determine what specific quantitative and qualitative factors appeared most frequently in all of the stocks. It was also necessary to determine when the identification of those factors could have been put to best use during the upward price movement of the stock.

The review encompassed the years since World War II and continued through recent years. Logically, this time period seemed to divide itself into two segments: from the end of World War II to the beginning of the Vietnam buildup in 1965, and from 1966 to 1981.

THE POSTWAR ERA

The postwar era was characterized by consecutively high periods of commodity inflation (1945, 1946) accompanied by persistently low price earnings ratios (see Appendix B), followed by a war expansion (Korea 1950 to 1953). Shortly thereafter, the country saw another recession—low inflation and even lower interest rates. Then, in the late 50s, the economy turned upward and price earnings ratios advanced sharply. This era ended with the enormous buildup of national budget deficits to finance social programs and to fight the war in Vietnam. These deficits and the huge increase in the money supply that followed were soon reflected in surging inflation and interest rates.

The 10-period following the 1957-58 recession produced many stocks that performed dramatically and persist to this day as viable investments (although most have already passed through the "super stock" stage of their lives). For the shrewd investor, 1958 was a good year to invest. Corporate earnings and stocks were down, pessimism was rampant, and, in general, prices did not appear cheap.

In the next table, 10 selected stocks are listed alphabetically along with the 1958 markets from which each might have been identified as a prime capital gains candidate. Also shown are the earnings and dividends in 1958 and, again, 10 years later. The 1958 stock prices shown were obtainable at the time. The 1968 price is that of the original stock, without adjusting for stock splits or dividends.

This table illustrates the important role sharply higher earnings and P/E multiples can play in a super stock portfolio. The higher stock price resulting is, of course, the investor's primary objective. However, the added benefit of growing dividends should not be overlooked. The table shows, for example, that the meager $2.60 IBM dividend in 1958 grew to a more respectable 5.4-percent annual return by 1968. Today, those same investors are enjoying a 30-percent return each year on that original investment. And, incredible as it may seem, Xerox investors are receiving, annually, nearly *three times* their original investment just from the dividend alone.

Clearly, dividend growth of this magnitude would not have been possible without the reinvestment (plowback) of profits in earlier years. Yet, when reviewing the table, the high payout ratio of Emery Air Freight stands out. How can a company grow as rapidly as Emery and still pay such a generous dividend at the same time? The answer is simple, after a little analysis. During this period, Emery was primarily a service business without serious competition, not very capital-intensive, and without the need to own much equipment. Therefore, the company's return on equity was very high (47 percent in 1968), which permitted a generous payout during those years. As long as Emery's ROE remained high, investors could expect a healthy earned growth rate *and* generous dividends.

DIVIDEND RETURNS FROM
SELECTED HIGH PERFORMANCE STOCKS
(1958-1968)

Company	Where Traded in 1958	Avg. Price 1958	1958 EPS	1958 Div.	1958 Yield	Avg. Price 1968	1968 EPS	1968 Div.	% of Original Investment
Avon Products	OTC	$ 61	$ 3.36	$1.45	2.4%	$1,169	$ 22.32	$14.40	23.5%
Baxter Products	OTC	32	2.42	0.74	2.3%	705	13.28	2.72	8.4%
Black & Decker	NYSE	48	3.16	1.70	3.6%	322	12.90	6.30	13.2%
Bristol-Myers	NYSE	65	4.38	2.15	3.3%	857	23.52	13.20	20.1%
Emery Air Freight	ASE	15	0.72	0.55	3.6%	266	5.76	3.72	24.4%
International Business Machines	NYSE	426	10.65	2.60	0.6%	2,903	68.35	23.04	5.4%
Johnson & Johnson	NYSE	116	5.95	2.05	1.8%	684	20.48	4.88	4.2%
Minnesota Mining & Manufacturing	NYSE	95	2.58	1.20	1.3%	301	8.91	4.35	4.6%
Nalco Chemical	OTC	37	2.83	1.25	3.4%	405	10.64	4.24	11.5%
Xerox (Haloid)	OTC	72	1.96	0.80	1.1%	5,576	103.80	28.80	40.1%

Recall the *Earned Growth Rate* formula from Chapter 3:

$$\text{Earned Growth Rate} = \frac{\text{Annual earnings } less \text{ annual dividends}}{\text{Book value (beginning of the year)}}$$

Here, then, is another definition of a super stock: "A company showing a return on equity high enough to eventually produce significant dividends."

THE POST-1966 PERIOD

The year 1966 was selected as the starting point of the second period since it marked the beginning of the inflation speedup that created a host of problems in the 1970s and early 1980s. This period was a difficult one for most companies. It was punctuated in 1973 and 1974 by a quadrupling of oil prices, double-digit inflation, rising interest rates, and a sharp recession. Even so, companies exhibiting rising earnings usually had those earnings reflected in rising stock prices despite all the economic problems of the period. The deep recession and stock market decline of 1974 set the stage for a whole new group of companies oriented toward natural resources or in new industries unthought of in the 1960s.

Among top market performers of the post-1966 period were the following seven representative stocks. Most enjoyed a substantial recovery from the lows of 1974.

Name	Where Traded	1966 Cost	1972 High	1974 Low	1982 Value
Block (H&R)	OTC•NYSE	$21	$420	$ 53	$ 380
Cox Broadcasting	NYSE	35	102	18	288
Digital Equipment	OTC•ASE•NYSE	26	309	147	783
Hewlett-Packard	NYSE	46	176	104	320
McDonald's Corp.	OTC•NYSE	25	963	269	812
Schlumberger	NYSE	50	425	331	1,276
Tandy Corp.	NYSE	15	98	20	2,176

Note: Prices are unadjusted for stock splits.

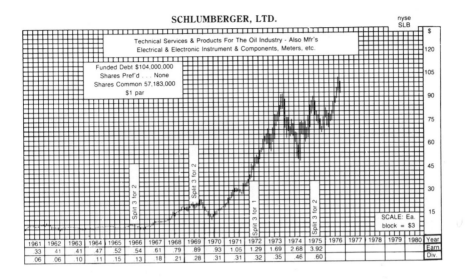

SCHLUMBERGER, LTD.

nyse
SLB

Technical Services & Products For The Oil Industry - Also Mfr's
Electrical & Electronic Instrument & Components, Meters, etc.

Funded Debt $104,000,000
Shares Pref'd . . . None
Shares Common 57,183,000
$1 par

SCALE: Ea.
block = $3

	1961	1962	1963	1964	1965	1966	1967	1968	1969	1970	1971	1972	1973	1974	1975	1976	1977	1978	1979	1980	
Year																					
Earn	33	.41	.41	47	52	.54	.61	79	.89	.93	1.05	1.29	1.69	2.68	3.92						
Div.	.06	.06	.10	.11	.15	.13	.18	21	.28	.31	.31	.32	.35	.46	.60						

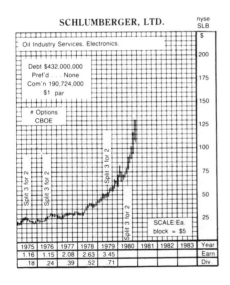

SCHLUMBERGER, LTD.

nyse
SLB

Oil Industry Services, Electronics.

Debt $432,000,000
Pref'd . . . None
Com'n 190,724,000
$1 par

Options
CBOE

SCALE:Ea.
block = $5

	1975	1976	1977	1978	1979	1980	1981	1982	1983	
Year										
Earn	1.16	1.15	2.08	2.63	3.45					
Div.	18	.24	.39	52	.71					

Schlumberger (pronouced Schlum-ber-shay) stock proved to be one of the big winners of the 1970's, rising nearly 2,000% in ten years. Clearly, this oil service company was at the right place at the right time!

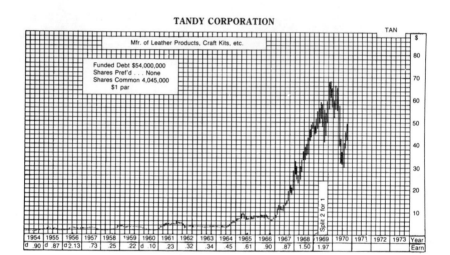

Look closely at both Tandy charts. Notice how an investor's perspective
can change with time. The frightening 1969-70 plunge lost its significance
in later years. By 1982, the stock was nearly $80 ($640 before adjusting for
splits since 1969)!

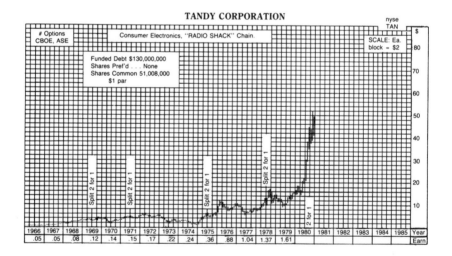

But not all that glitters is gold. Here are a few of the "new" growth stocks of the 1960s that became the "busts" even before the great bear market of the 1970s:

GROWTH STARS OF THE SIXTIES

	1960-70 High	Market Price September, 1972
Alpine Geophysical	44	1 3/4
Ampex	49 7/8	6 3/8
Arlan's Department Stores	40 7/8	3 1/2
Ecological Science	28 3/4	Trading Suspended
Electronic Memories	43 3/4	4 1/8
FAS International	82	1/8
Four Seasons Nursing	102	Trading Suspended
Ionics	61 1/2	16 3/4
Ipco Hospital Supply	37 3/4	8 7/8
Leasco	57 1/4	21 5/8
L-T-V	169 1/2	10
Management Assistance	45	3/8
Mattel	52	14 7/8
Memorex	174	17 7/8
National Student Marketing	79	3/4
Potter Instruments	46	9 1/4
Pueblo International	26 3/8	6 7/8
Savin Business Machines	73	15 3/4
Tyco	68	16 3/8
University Computing	187	13 3/8

The tabulation is more eloquent than thousands of words regarding the "buy and hold" strategy, which claims that all you have to do is identify, buy, and then hold a growth stock to become rich. What the experts were saying in the early 1970s was that established growth records are usually good buys for the long pull even if their price earnings ratios are high. That's fine as long as the company is still growing rapidly. Of course, few of these ever met our super stock qualifications in the first place.

One of the more memorable "busts" began in late 1972—Levitz Furniture, one of the so-called "concept" stocks of the early 1970s.

It was the first company with a new type of retailing: combination warehouse-showroom-retail stores that sold nationally advertised brands of furniture. These products were priced lower than in conventional furniture stores and the stores were big, with plenty of showroom and warehouse space. It was an innovative selling tool in a hidebound industry.

The results were spectacular in the furniture business and in the stock market. The stock could have been purchased at 13 in January, 1971. It quickly rose to 60 in mid-1972. You had to be quick, though. The stock stopped abruptly and then declined to a low of 17 that same year. It eventually hit 2 in 1974. Levitz may have been a growth company of sorts, but it could not maintain the earnings power it took years to build in a traditionally low-margin business with rising competition and difficult economic times.

These experiences provide yet another definition of super stock: "A stock that is rising for sound, long-term fundamental reasons; not just a temporary move in a bull market." Most importantly we are seeking a sustainability of earning power, not just a flash in the pan. We are looking for more than just a super price-performance; we want stocks at "never-again" prices!

Finally, looking back over the past 30 or 40 years, there is still one more lesson to be learned: *Super stocks can be found at any time.* For example, the 5 years between 1976 and 1982 were not especially bright for the stock market. During these years, the U.S. encountered a recession, inflation and unemployment rose to extremely high levels, the prime rate climbed above 20 percent, and U.S. prestige hit its lowest point when its embassy was overrun by a second-rate country.

In 1976, the Dow Jones Industrial Average high was 1027. Not surprisingly, the index stood at 875 at the end of 1981, about 15 percent lower. However, during this same period, the stock of an automation equipment company called Computervision Corporation advanced more than 4,000 percent. A $2,000 investment in Computervision at its highest price in 1976 had a market value of $85,300 as 1981 drew to a close.

PROFILES OF SOME MAJOR SUPER STOCKS

The following are historical overviews of major super stocks. There are differences among the companies, but most share certain common characteristics that become evident in retrospect.

IBM

IBM is, of course, one of the premier super stocks. In the mid-1920s, an investor could have bought shares in a growing company called Computing-Tabulating-Recording. At that time, this fledgling office supplier had 120,000 shares outstanding. Today, that company is IBM, a business that made millions for its shareholders. For example, an investor purchasing IBM at the highest price in 1957, before a sharp 25-percent decline later that year, would have paid $376½ (a P/E of 48.7). In 1957, about 30 percent of IBM's $7.73 earnings per share was paid to shareholders in dividends. Not adjusting for splits (there have been no fewer than seven since then), IBM stock reached $3,081 in February, 1973! The annual dividend rate currently is equivalent to $145 per share on the stock purchased in 1957—a 39 percent return on the original investment *each year!*

Over the years, IBM's stock rose for sound, long-term fundamental reasons. The company moved from a small, fast-growing office equipment manufacturer into the then new field of computers in the early 1950s. Management made a superb bet by concentrating on building a marketing and service organization for IBM equipment. The company soon established dominance. The fact that the computer business proved to be one of the fastest-growing industry segments of the post-World War II period only confirmed management's brilliant moves and enhanced the results.

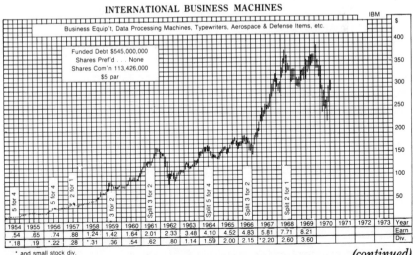

INTERNATIONAL BUSINESS MACHINES

Business Equip't, Data Processing Machines, Typewriters, Aerospace & Defense Items, etc.

Funded Debt $545,000,000
Shares Pref'd . . . None
Shares Com'n 113,426,000
$5 par

	1954	1955	1956	1957	1958	1959	1960	1961	1962	1963	1964	1965	1966	1967	1968	1969	1970	1971	1972	1973 Year
Earn	.54	.65	.74	.88	1.24	1.42	1.64	2.01	2.33	3.48	4.10	4.52	4.83	5.81	7.71	8.21				
Div.	*.18	.19	*.22	.28	*.31	.36	.54	.62	.80	1.14	1.59	2.00	2.15	*2.20	2.60	3.60				

* and small stock div.

(continued)

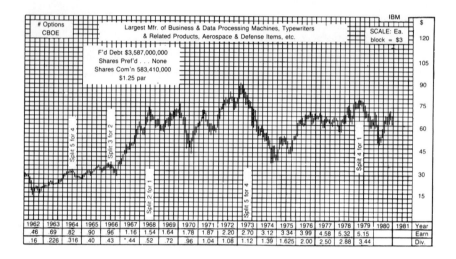

	1962	1963	1964	1965	1966	1967	1968	1969	1970	1971	1972	1973	1974	1975	1976	1977	1978	1979	1980	1981	Year
Earn	.46	.69	.82	.90	.96	1.16	1.54	1.64	1.78	1.87	2.20	2.70	3.12	3.34	3.99	4.58	5.32	5.15			
Div	.16	.226	.316	.40	.43	*.44	.52	.72	.96	1.04	1.08	1.12	1.39	1.625	2.00	2.50	2.88	3.44			

And, as these two charts illustrate, a stockholder can benefit when the P/E multiple is stable or expanding (as it did in the 1954 to 1969 period when IBM earnings grew at 20 percent per year). After 1969, earnings continued to grow, but at a slower rate of 12 percent annually, and the stock did nothing. That "magic combination" is important. When a company is in its slow-down (maturity) phase, a shrinking P/E multiple can hurt long-term investment performance.

Few market observers are unaware of the fact that a P/E of 40 in 1982 was a much more rare phenomenon than it was 10 years earlier. The reasons, experts tell us, are many—higher interest rates, higher inflation, slower earnings growth, etc. At this writing, one thing seems reasonably certain: the overall direction of most P/E multiples will be more favorable in the 1980s than it was in the 1970s, which argues well for future super stock investors. While absolute levels of P/E's are certainly not to be ignored, it is the *trend*, up or down, that will greatly influence the final results.

3M

Minnesota Mining & Manufacturing started tenuously in 1902 as a venture to quarry a mineral called corundum at Crystal Bay, Minnesota. The mineral was then to be sold to eastern manufacturers for use as a new, improved abrasive. After the company's near-failure, Edgar B. Ober and Lucius P. Ordway converted an old flour mill into a sandpaper manufacturing facility. By 1906, the new enterprise was

3M's first plant located on the shore of Lake Superior at Crystal Bay, Minnesota.

finally enjoying its initial orders, although corundum was eventually proved worthless as a commercial abrasive.

William L. McKnight was hired as assistant bookkeeper in May, 1907. At age 24 in 1911, he was appointed sales manager and, soon thereafter, general manager. In 1914, sales were more than $200,000 and climbing, due to innovative sales programs instituted by McKnight. "Talk to the people using our sandpaper," he would say. William McKnight was a major force in the company during its first 50 years.

William L. McKnight (2nd from left) welcomes employees to the board room when he was named Chairman of the Board in 1949.

Until the company moved to St. Paul in 1910, 3M leased an old flour mill in Duluth where sandpaper was manufactured. Circa 1908.

One of the first consumer packages for 3M products: Household Wetordry water proof sandpaper.

Bing Crosby's dislike of doing "live" radio shows led to the growth of recorded commercial broadcasts and rapid expansion of "Scotch" sound recording tape, which 3M introduced in the late 1940s.

3M introduced the first presensitized offset litho plate in the 1950s.

Lewis W. Lehr, like others before him, rose "through the ranks" to become Chairman of the Board of 3M. He was closely associated with the development of 3M's health care business and is shown here (right) in pilot plant work involving packaging of surgical drapes in 1950.

MINNESOTA MINING & MFG. COMPANY

nyse
MMM

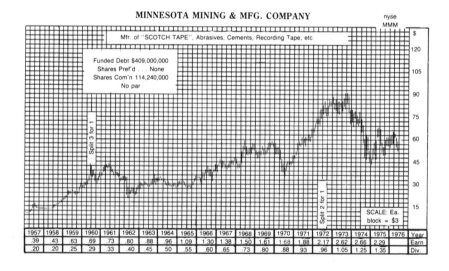

Mfr. of "SCOTCH TAPE", Abrasives, Cements, Recording Tape, etc.

Funded Debt $409,000,000
Shares Pref'd . . . None
Shares Com'n 114,240,000
No par

Split 3 for 1

Split 2 for 1

SCALE: Ea.
block = $3

Year	1957	1958	1959	1960	1961	1962	1963	1964	1965	1966	1967	1968	1969	1970	1971	1972	1973	1974	1975	1976
Earn	.39	.43	.63	.69	.73	.80	.88	.96	1.09	1.30	1.38	1.50	1.61	1.68	1.88	2.17	2.62	2.66	2.29	
Div.	.20	.20	.25	.29	.33	.40	.45	.50	.55	.60	.65	.73	.80	.88	.93	.96	1.05	1.25	1.35	

The reorganization instituted by Chief Executive McKnight in 1948 set the stage for substantial growth in the 1950s and beyond. That year, the company was divided into seven major divisions: Adhesives; Roofing Granules; Coated Abrasives; Pressure-Sensitive Tapes; Reflective Products; Color and Chemical; and Electrical Insulation/Sound-Recording Tapes. This company's continuing success over the years has been, in part, due to its corporate organization. To this day, 3M views itself as a collection of many small-growth businesses rather than one huge enterprise.

As 3M ended 1952, its 50th anniversary year, sales were approaching $200 million, and although profit margins were very healthy, earnings had been flat since 1949. Why? To those who knew of 3M's record and took time to look more carefully, this was clearly a transitional period. New products were being developed, new plants were under construction, and only one year earlier, 3M made its first direct entry into international markets. In short, 3M was poised and ready for another period of growth and had plenty of room to do so.

And grow it did! 3M's earnings progress continued uninterrupted for the next 22 years. A 100-share purchase of 3M stock in 1952 for $4,200 would have been valued at $109,200 at its peak 21 years later. Today, those same shares purchased in 1952 are enjoying an annual dividend of $4,464!

Xerox Corporation

Xerox, a major manufacturer of reproduction equipment, is yet another generic term for "super stock." People are constantly talking about finding *another* Xerox in the same way King Arthur's knights must have talked about the holy grail.

Just after the turn of the century, George C. Beidler, a clerk in an abstract office in Oklahoma City, invented the Rectigraph machine for the primary purpose of developing an efficient method to copy legal documents. The resulting business, the Rectigraph Company, soon thereafter moved to Rochester, New York. In 1935, it was acquired by The Haloid Company (founded in April, 1906). For a short time, the Company was known as Haloid Xerox, Inc. and in June, 1961 was renamed Xerox Corporation.

Meanwhile, in the late 1930s, physicist Chester F. Carlson began independent experiments on photoconductors—materials that conduct electricity, especially when exposed to light. In 1940, Mr. Carlson re-

Two key executives during the years of Xerox Corporation's fastest growth are pictured here with the Xerox 914, introduced in 1960. Joseph C. Wilson (right) was President from 1946 until 1966, when he was appointed Chairman of the Board. His successor as Chairman, C. Peter McColough, joined Haloid in 1954, was named Vice President-Sales in 1960, and was elected President in 1966.

ceived his first patent on a transfer electrostatic process. In the few years following, he was turned away by several companies including IBM, Eastman Kodak, and RCA. In 1944, Battelle Memorial Institute agreed to further his research efforts and, 3 years later, The Haloid Company, in addition to its own work, began sponsoring Battelle research on the process. In 1948, after many improvements, Battelle licensed its patent rights to the process to Haloid, which, in 1950, introduced its first commercial xerographic machine—the manually operated Model D Copier.

In the 1950s Haloid Xerox proceeded to purchase Battelle patents for cash and stock and, in an agreement effective January, 1959, acquired all improvement patents and patent applications relating to xerography owned by Battelle. Final payment under the agreement was made by Xerox in 1966 bringing the total consideration paid to $63.7 million ($9.1 million in cash and $54.6 million in stock valued at the dates of issue). In 1960, the company introduced its first major product—the Xerox 914 which was the beginning of a revolution in office copying. For the first time, reasonably high-quality, dry copies were made automatically on ordinary paper.

In the early 1960s alone, an investment in Xerox would have doubled, then tripled, then quadrupled. In 1972, Haloid stock was selling

XEROX CORPORATION

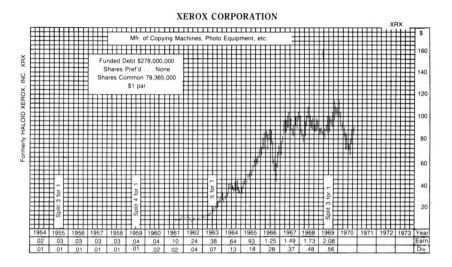

XRX

Formerly HALOID XEROX, INC. XRX

Mfr. of Copying Machines, Photo Equipment, etc.

Funded Debt $278,000,000
Shares Pref'd . . . None
Shares Common 78,365,000
$1 par

Split 3 for 1 | Split 4 for 1 | 5 for 1 | Split 3 for 1

1954	1955	1956	1957	1958	1959	1960	1961	1962	1963	1964	1965	1966	1967	1968	1969	1970	1971	1972	1973	Year
.02	.03	.03	.03	.03	.04	.04	.10	.24	.38	.64	.93	1.25	1.49	1.73	2.08					Earn
.01	.01	.01	.01	.01	.01	.02	.02	.04	.07	.13	.18	.28	.37	.48	.56					Div.

above $170 a share compared to an adjusted cost of $1¾ in the late 1950s.

Walt Disney Productions

The Walt Disney experience shows that a company doesn't necessarily need technology to be a super stock.

A combination of enduring cartoon characters like Mickey Mouse and Donald Duck, a timeless film library bursting with fairy tale classics like *Snow White, Cinderella,* and *Pinocchio,* and the potential of its theme parks was all the magic Disney needed to become a super stock.

Until the opening of Disneyland at Anaheim, California in 1955, the company's profits were derived primarily from the production and distribution of motion picture films for theaters and television, as well as other entertainment products. In fact, ever since the company's founding in 1938, Disney's films, comic strips, book materials, and licensed products have long delighted young and old alike.

By the early 1960s, the direction of the company's fortune was becoming clear as the Disneyland success was being translated into substantial sales and earnings gains. The opening of Disney World in Orlando, Florida in October, 1971 did not go unnoticed by Wall Street. Its anticipation in the late 1960s and the revenue contribution that began in 1972 was not inconsequential. The stock's P/E ratio climbed from

DISNEY (WALT) PRODUCTIONS

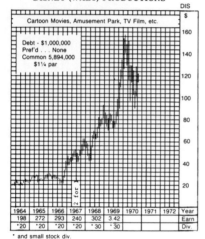

1964	1965	1966	1967	1968	1969	1970	1971	1972	Year
198	272	293	240	302	3.42				Earn.
'20	'20	'20	'20	' 30	' 30				Div.

* and small stock div.

Investors who bought Disney at the high in 1970 were unhappy with the 40% + decline within six months. However, the stock was experiencing only a brief pause on its way to $496 ($124 after two 2 for 1 stock splits).

10.7 to more than 70 times its earnings between 1963 to 1973. At the same time, revenues increased from $81.9 million to $328.8 million and profits zoomed from $6.6 million to $47.8 million. Adjusted for stock splits and stock dividends, earnings advanced from 36 cents to $1.61 per share, and the value of a 100-share $4,125 investment in 1963 rose to $123,875 within 10 years.

Johnson & Johnson

Robert Wood Johnson and his two brothers, James Wood and Edward Mead Johnson, formed their new enterprise on the belief that "there ought to be a better way." The business, which began in 1886 on the fourth floor of a small factory building in New Brunswick, New Jersey, was incorporated as Johnson & Johnson in 1887. By 1892, the company developed a superior production method for dressings that involved a continuous dry-sterilization process. Indeed, Robert Wood Johnson's idea for a new type of surgical dressing, wrapped and sealed in separate packages, and ready for immediate use, was truly a "better way."

Under the leadership of three men—Robert Wood Johnson, brother James Wood Johnson, and son General Robert Wood Johnson—the company emerged as the giant in its field.

In late 1959, as the company's 72nd year was drawing to a close, an investor in Johnson & Johnson could look back a few years with a great deal of satisfaction. The stock was selling in the low 60s, triple the price of only 5 years earlier. After all, the company was making progress; it was the world's largest manufacturer of surgical dressings, including its well-known "Band-Aid" brand adhesive bandages. At the annual meeting, management was telling shareholders that sales were about 50 percent above the figures of 5 years ago, while, at the same time, profits climbed 55 percent. For 1959, Johnson & Johnson reported earnings of $1.61 per share on sales of $301 million. Now, after a stock split and the addition of McNeil Laboratories, a producer of ethical drugs acquired earlier that year, there were 5,923,000 shares outstanding.

Disneyland at Anaheim, California

© Walt Disney Productions

Walt Disney World at Orlando, Florida

Robert Wood Johnson joined with his two brothers to form Johnson & Johnson. He served as president between 1886 and 1910.

James Wood Johnson succeeded his brother as president in 1910 and was head of the company until 1932.

With the stock selling at nearly 40 times earnings and the prospect of slower earnings growth in 1960, might this, perhaps, be the time to sell?

A closer look at 1959, however, made this investment appear a great deal more attractive than figures in the newspapers suggested. The company's foreign profits, which were growing nicely, were not consolidated. This meant that the reported figures were somewhat understated. Moreover, promising new products were being introduced regularly, the company was very profitable with a large amount of working capital and no debt. Up to this point, the management had an outstanding record of accomplishment. Why should it not continue? Could sales not reach $600 million, or more, in the foreseeable future?

Johnson & Johnson's growth did, in fact, continue. Today, the company's sales are close to $6 billion! In 1967, and again in 1970, the stock was split 3 for 1. Johnson & Johnson stock reached a peak in 1972 of $133, an equivalent price of nearly $1,200 for that same

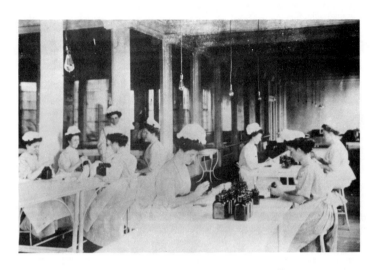

Cotton packaging at Johnson & Johnson in 1910.

General Robert Wood Johnson, son of company's first president, was an employee at Johnson & Johnson as a young man. He was, in part, responsible for the company's expansion into international markets in the early 1920s. "The General" was president from 1932 until 1963, and remained active in the company until his death in 1968.

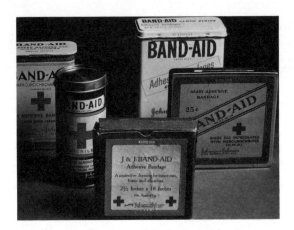

The "Band-Aid" Brand Adhesive Bandage was invented in 1920 by a Johnson & Johnson employee, Earle E. Dickson.

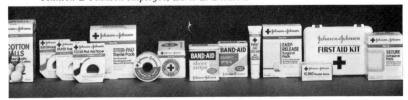

JOHNSON & JOHNSON

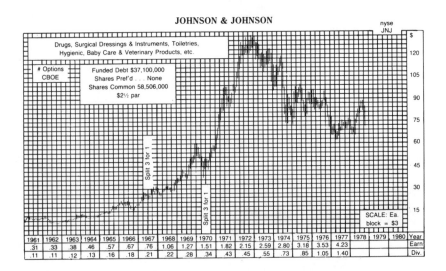

nyse
JNJ

Drugs, Surgical Dressings & Instruments, Toiletries, Hygienic, Baby Care & Veterinary Products, etc.

Options
CBOE

Funded Debt $37,100,000
Shares Pref'd . . . None
Shares Common 58,506,000
$2½ par

Split 3 for 1

Split 3 for 1

SCALE: Ea.
block = $3

Year	1961	1962	1963	1964	1965	1966	1967	1968	1969	1970	1971	1972	1973	1974	1975	1976	1977	1978	1979	1980
Earn	.31	.33	.38	.46	.57	.67	.76	1.06	1.27	1.51	1.82	2.15	2.59	2.80	3.18	3.53	4.23			
Div.	.11	.11	.12	.13	.16	.18	.21	.22	.28	.34	.43	.45	.55	.73	.85	1.05	1.40			

stock held in 1959! In the perspective of the preceding 20 years, and with continuing growth still in prospect, people in 1972 had to be asking: "With the multiple at 60 times, how high is high?" And, as experienced investors today know, a little man does not come around ringing a bell, even for super stocks!

CHARACTERISTICS OF WELL-PERFORMING STOCKS

Although super stocks can pop up in any industry, many of the best-performing stocks of the past have some technological orientation in their product line. Nevertheless, as Charles Allmon, head of "The Growth Stock Outlook," an investment advisory service that concentrates on small and rapidly growing companies, points out: "It isn't necessary to have a technology hardware stock to do well . . . nor is it desirable in relationship to risk. You can buy value and be safe and secure in knowing that that value will eventually be reflected in the market price."

All true and all to the good. But a review of the best performers does suggest that technology, more than not, is a better bet.

In addition to size and a leaning toward technology, the better-performing stocks seem to possess a majority of the following characteristics:

- A leading position in an attractive industry.

- A proprietary product or service that will do an essential job better or cheaper than the competition.

- Strong, progressive, and research-minded management.

- An ability to develop new products and penetrate new markets.

- Rising sales accompanied by continuing growth in unit demand.

- A healthy return on stockholders' equity, with improvement over the years.

- A relatively low labor cost.

- The means to finance future growth internally with minimal reliance on capital markets.

- An ability to produce high profit margins on sales with the immediate prospect of rising profit margins.

- The ability to raise prices as costs go up, without attracting political opposition.
- A strong financial position (low debt).
- A high plowback ratio of earnings.
- Conservative, sensible accounting.
- A limited exposure to environmental, social, and political pressures.
- Reasonable freedom from import competition.
- Rising earnings per share relative to most other stocks.
- The stock should not yet be too popular among the institutions.
- Rising dividends, although the payout ratio (amount of dividends paid out of earnings) should be fairly low to allow for a generous plowback of earnings.
- A stable or rising price earnings multiple.

Each of these 19 characteristics has something going for it. And each, by itself, at the right time and in the right market, can move a stock's price up. But a careful examination of the "super stock" successes in all the market periods described thus far gradually eliminates characteristic after characteristic. Not every super stock on the list had conservative, sensible accounting. Nor did each of our winners have top-notch proprietary products, services or skills. As a matter of fact, careful examination of all super stocks eliminated all but nine characteristics that were common to all super stocks. None had less than these nine!

1). Small to medium size.
2). Rising unit sales volume.
3). Rising pretax profit margins.
4). Above-average, and improving, return on stockholders' equity.
5). Strong earnings per share growth relative to most stocks.
6). A low payout ratio with rising dividends.
7). Low debt ratio.
8). Low institutional holdings.
9). Increasing price earnings multiple.

Each of these nine characteristics—so important to our search for the "super stock"— will be described in detail in the next chapter.

5
Out of the
Forest, Into The Trees

MOST SUPER STOCKS EXPERIENCE A POINT WHERE MANAGEMENT IS reasonably well seasoned and, at the same time, the company has reached a good size (that is, a sales volume large enough to be generating a useful cash flow of meaningful proportions). Moreover, the company, or the market it is serving, is usually not yet quite large enough to attract major competition. At such a point, the company is hungry—hungry for people, for more working space, and for new ideas. The company is simply hungry for new worlds to conquer.

SIZE OF THE COMPANY

Accordingly, we are seeking businesses that are on the threshold of fast growth. These are companies with annual sales of $25 million to $500 million, depending on the industry. Companies this size are in the most volatile segment of the corporate spectrum since it is especially demanding of managerial skills.

These threshold companies are extremely explosive and can spurt ahead by finding and exploiting a market niche too small or specialized to attract billion-dollar enterprises. But the risk is also great. Typically, the company is more vulnerable to industry downturns due to less diversification, more in need on costly debt financing, and shorter on staying power in a recession. These companies must evolve as they grow. A small company can remain under its founder's close supervision and still prosper by offering a single line of relatively simple products sold over a limited geographic area to a smaller number of customers. By contrast, with growth, there are also difficult management problems such as delegation of authority, as well as a need for planning and market research. All require new layers of management. And that is "another world" to many entrepreneurs.

Each economic shakeout sees a number of these companies fail completely or merge with unfavorable terms just to survive. But others continue to grow at high rates, even in a difficult economic environment. One important factor for survival and growth rate continuation is maintaining profit margins in an economic downturn. These successful companies can, and usually do, react quickly by raising prices to pass along costs and by weeding out less profitable items. They also display "the entrepreneurial courage" to get full price for what they sell. They search out items that are less sensitive to price competition and focus their attention on these items.

Additionally, the successful "threshold companies" also stay close to their market niches. Diversification spreads the risk but also dilutes profitability. Rather than overextending themselves or risking a head-on collision with more powerful competitors, the successful company concentrates on market segments that huge corporations often ignore.

Finally, a threshold company's chief executive officer is often a crucial element. Unlike a giant corporation, where the chief executive is usually bolstered by stable echelons of trained managers, a smaller company—for better or worse—is greatly shaped by its top man or woman. Much depends on that executive's ability to adapt himself and the company to the changing demands of growth. But overall, the most important task is to sustain top management's drive and to maintain the company's vitality as long as possible.

Size, then, is one of the crucial characteristics of our super stock. Not too big, not too small. We want a threshold company with sales and earnings ready to accelerate.

This specific size range also tends to minimize our risk since we are not investing in newly born companies. We have seen the company prove itself in the real world for a few years. This means, of course, that we have also given up some of the initial gain enjoyed by the founders of the company. That's fine. They've earned it by taking the biggest risk. But even bigger gains are about to occur if we're right about the company and the stock. Explosive sales and earnings growth will result in significantly higher stock prices once investors begin to recognize the potential of our super stock.

How do we identify both the company and its "threshold point"?

Recall the corporate life cycle discussed earlier. At the takeoff stage when the value of the company's services or products are perceived in the marketplace, sales begin to increase dramatically. Earnings will tend to increase even faster as the power of sales leverage begins to display itself. This is the ideal point to buy the stock. Sales and earnings over the past several years have demonstrated the company's viability. The company is no longer completely vulnerable and mistakes in investment timing can be absorbed more readily. While the initial stock investors (including venture capitalists) have probably doubled or tripled their money, there is still plenty of capital appreciation left if the company continues its course. Furthermore, although the investment risk is quite high, there is substantially less risk than one or two years before. This stage also represents the period in which shrewd investors are beginning to analyze the stock and a few institutions have begun to invest.

The sharp curving climb to stage 4 (maturity) constitutes the period of maximum gain. In stage 4, age is setting in and the growth will taper. This is also the period when the major institutions have already become or are becoming stockholders. Newspapers will call it a "glamour" stock while others may call it a blue chip. No matter what the name, growth in the stock price will probably continue, but at a slower pace. Note, too, that these "super stock" phases may last long periods of time—totaling 5, 10, or 15 years. At stage 3, the future appears bright and the company's earnings potential seems unlimited. By looking for stocks of "threshold" companies, we are inventorying them before the majority of institutions recognize their potential. At some point, when institutional investors finally begin to buy our super stock, we, as investors with long-term perspective, will gladly enjoy the ride.

UNIT SALES VOLUME

Rising sales volume is essential to any growth company. (Here, the term "sales" refers to net sales—the actual sales and/or revenues after deducting allowances, returns, and cash discounts taken by customers. However, this is usually not a crucial distinction.) How fast should sales be rising? As a general rule, growth should not be less than an annual rate of 12 to 15 percent during a strong economic year. Furthermore, the prospects of 15 to 20 percent (or more) annually should not be out of reach.

On the other hand, a rising sales trend does not always mean a company is enjoying greater prosperity. Sales might be going up, but overall expenses to produce those products or services might be going up even faster. It is possible for a company to survive this squeeze temporarily by cutting expenses or by producing more with the same, or less, labor and equipment. But without sales growth, in today's environment, a company is ultimately doomed. Not only are rising sales essential to corporate profits, they are also a thermometer of corporate health. A rising sales trend means the company's products and services are winning greater acceptance with the customer and that the company's marketing efforts are successful.

There is, however, a catch when using rising sales volume as a sought-after characteristic of a super stock. The best way to describe this "trap" is to offer an example. Let's look at XYZ Corporation's record of increasing sales:

XYZ CORPORATION
Net Sales in $ 000's

	Year 1	Year 2	Year 3	Year 4	Year 5
Reported Net Sales	$10,000	$12,000	$15,000	$17,000	$20,000
% Change	—	+ 20%	+ 25%	+ 13%	+ 18%

A pretty good sales record. Right? Net sales doubled in 4 years. That's an annual growth rate of nearly 20 percent! But remember, the sales figure also includes prices. We should look at these sales figures and compare them to the actual unit volume of products shipped. In this case, if the company sold 1 million units at $10 each in the first year, and 10 percent more, or 1,100,000 units in the second year, but dollar sales volume increased 20 percent, why the difference? Answer: an increase in prices. This could be a reflection of rising costs in an inflationary period.

If it happens again in the third, fourth, and fifth year, dollar sales will continue to rise faster than unit volume. And, frequently, price increases will adversely impact unit growth, or perhaps hide a slowdown that might already be occurring in unit sales. It is possible that, despite a reported increase in sales, XYZ Corporation has lost momentum in the marketing of its products or services. This could be an early danger sign of a weakening competitive situation. Had the XYZ Corporation reported the sales and unit volume figures shown below, the conclusion might be less favorable:

XYZ CORPORATION

	Year 1	Year 2	Year 3	Year 4	Year 5
Reported Net Sales	$10,000	$12,000	$15,000	$17,000	$20,000
% Change	—	+ 20%	+ 25%	+ 13%	+ 18%
Unit Sales Volume	1,000	1,100	1,200	1,250	1,225
% Change	—	+ 10%	+ 9%	+ 4%	– 2%
Unit Price	$10.00	$10.91	$12.50	$13.60	$16.33
% Price Change	—	+ 9.1%	+ 14.6%	+ 8.8%	+ 20.1%

The point is that unit sales growth is one of the most important characteristics separating the ordinary growth company from the super stock. Sales volume in dollars is a good initial indicator, but a strong showing in unit growth is more conclusive.

Without knowing a company's unit shipments, there is an easy, shortcut way to measure unit growth. By adjusting the company's reported dollar sales figures by the overall inflation rate of the economy (i.e., using the annual percentage change of the Consumer Price Index—see Appendix A), an investor can make an "educated guess" of the unit growth, If, for example, reported dollar sales advanced 19 percent and CPI increased 8 percent that year, the unit growth would be approximately 11 percent. This is, admittedly, a rough calculation. And, without care, it could be misleading. However, short of obtaining figures directly from the company, this approach is the most effective method.

One further note of caution when analyzing large companies with extensive overseas operations: Sales can be greatly influenced by changes in international currency rates. Adjustments can be made quite easily using the figures usually found in the footnotes of the annual reports. However, for most "threshold" companies, international sales are still only a small, growing part of the business (and, in fact, just one more reason for substantial growth in the years ahead).

RISING PROFIT MARGIN

A company's profit margin can be defined as the relationship of income (profit) before, or after, taxes to net sales. If a company, Alpha Corporation, had net sales of $35.6 million and if the total expense of generating those sales (production cost plus selling, administrative costs, etc.) was $28.7 million, then the company's profit before taxes would be $6.9 million. This would be a pretax profit margin of 19.5 percent ($6.9 million divided by $35.6 million).

The pretax margin reflects the efficiency of a company to extract a profit from each dollar of sales. Also, more than any other ratio or percentage, the pretax profit margin indicates just how profitable and effective a company has been within its industry. Most experts favor pretax profit margins as an analytical tool since the profitablity of one company can be compared against another without the variables of different tax rates.

As a general rule, very few super stocks have pretax profit margins below 10 to 12 percent. Once in the growth phase, a 15 to 20 percent (or more) margin is not unusual. For example, Alpha Corporation presented their income statement as follows:

ALPHA CORPORATION
Income Statement

	Year Ended December 31	
	Last Year	Year Before
Net Sales	$35,598,782	$30,945,236
Cost of Goods Sold	20,009,100	17,289,604
Gross Profit	$15,589,682	$13,655,632
Selling, Admin. & Gen'l. Expenses	9,370,600	8,678,577
Operating Profit	$ 6,219,082	$ 4,977,055
Profit Before Taxes	$ 6,954,136	$ 5,739,901
Pretax Profit Margin	19.5%	18.5%
Provision for Taxes	2,791,230	2,548,090
Net Profit	$ 4,162,906	$ 3,225,811

In this case, Alpha's pretax profit margin increased from 18.5 percent to 19.5 percent in the most recent year.

Put another way—if Alpha Corporation makes 19½ cents for every $1.00 of sales, we know that Alpha's management is doing a better job than the competition who might only be doing, say, 12 percent.

Profit margins tell us more eloquently than words that one company is operating much more efficiently than another. It is an affirmation of a company's skill in controlling the costs of doing business. The fact that Alpha's cost of goods sold is now proportionately higher than it was earlier is a point of concern and bears watching. But, overall, the company's profitability improved.

Not only are Alpha's sales rising, but management is also more skillful in capturing profits. Now we can compare Alpha to other companies in the industry and to the industry average each year to be sure Alpha is maintaining its profitability. If profit margins were drifting down rather than advancing, we might monitor the company's progress, hoping to spot the turnaround margins. Declining profit margins could be a temporary situation, due to the economy; unusual operating expenses related to a new, more efficient plant; or the startup of a new operation. Any of these could restore or enhance profit margins. If one of these is the explanation, fine. We'll watch and wait for the beginning of the turn and defer buying the stock until there are definite signs of improvement.

Sometimes getting a new plant up to speed takes longer than expected. So, we carefully plot the company's progress quarter-by-quarter to detect the beginning of the turnaround in margins. However, if we bought the stock on rising profit margins and then, suddenly, they declined, we would consider this to be a danger signal. The question then would be: Is this temporary? Do we have an unusual situation because of expansion, or a bad economy, or has management lost control of expenses? We might have misjudged the company. Is competition getting keener, requiring price cutting and heavier marketing expenses?

High pretax profit margins (above 10 to 15 percent) are desirable because they give a corporation the profits for further growth. But more important than the magnitude of the margins is the *trend* extending over several years. The trend must be level or rising. It should never be falling, unless from extremely high, unsustainable levels.

Earlier, it was noted that the profit margin is the relationship of income to net sales. But this takes into account only two of the three essential factors in a corporation meeting its profit objective: sales and expenses. The third is investment. A new plant increase of capacity by 20 percent requires substantial investment to achieve this 20 percent increase in sales. If profit margins were the only basis of measurement, many mutiproduct companies would give emphasis to product lines with high margins, but with low return on investment, rather than to those lines with high return on investment. As a result, reliance on the profit margin computation as a sole measurement for calculating profitability is misplaced.

The profit margin tells us how much profit is realized from sales but doesn't take into account the amount of investment required to produce those sales. Since investment in plant and equipment ultimately produces sales, we want to know how efficiently a company is utilizing invested funds. This brings us to the most important criterion: Rate of Return on Stockholders' Equity.

RETURN ON STOCKHOLDER'S EQUITY

Just as the profit margin percentage is a measure of management's efficiency in extracting profits from each sales dollar, the profit earned on the stockholders' investment is the indicator of management's efficiency in using the stockholders' funds remaining in the company. In other words, what has been management's productivity of capital?

The best way to measure "productivity of capital" is to track the profitability of the company's "Stockholders' Equity" (total assets less total liabilities), sometimes also called "Net Worth," by relating the company's profit to the level of stockholders' equity. In so doing, we can see just how successful management has been with the stockholders' money. This calculation is referred to as "Return on Stockholders' Equity," or simply, "Return on Equity." It is found in the following manner:

$$\frac{\text{Net profit after taxes}}{\text{Stockholders' Equity}} = \%\ \text{Return on Stockholders' Equity}$$

If the company has preferred stock, the return on equity is calculated by first deducting the preferred stock dividend from the net profit, and deducting the par value of the perferred stock from the stockholders' equity before dividing.

Furthermore, to be precise, when figuring return on equity, it is better to *average* the year-beginning and year-ending stockholders' equity rather than just using the year-end figure in the calculation. The net income was earned over an entire 12-month period. Therefore, it should be related to the *average* stockholders' equity rather than just the year-end figure. However, for the sake of simplicity and speed, the year-end stockholders' equity figure does suffice for a rough calculation.

If the principal goal of our target company is increasing profit, the purpose of retaining the profit is to enjoy a reasonable percentage return on the money management is investing for us. Otherwise, it should be paid out as dividends. Further, management has a responsibility to earn on the stockholders' capital *at least* that amount available on alternative investments. If the company cannot earn a *reasonable* return for investors, then they should be able to recover their money and put it to more productive uses themselves. They should ask management to forsake growth and return their investment as dividends.

But it is a rare corporate situation where the stockholders can jointly put such a question to management and receive a response. Typically, management will seek other avenues of growth, new areas of expansion or acquisitions rather than confess their inability to earn a market rate of return.

The historical returns for many listed companies, particularly in the steel industry, are woefully below market returns over long periods of time. These companies have persisted in pouring cash into low-return businesses for years, hoping for better times. They would have done better either paying out the cash to investors in the form of higher dividends or simply investing the money in Treasury Bills. In either case, the stockholder would have been better off. *But* you don't retain high-priced management to invest in Treasury Bills. So management continues to throw good money after bad. The result is usually disastrous for shareholders.

If you, as a stockholder, cannot convince management to return part of your accumulated profits or to invest in more favorable investment areas, take your money and run. You sell your stock and move elsewhere.

RETURN ON STOCKHOLDERS' EQUITY

Years	Steel Co. A	Steel Co. B	Steel Co. C	Average Interest on Treasury Bills
1	4.3%	—	4.5%	5.0%
2	4.3	4.2%	6.6	5.0
3	8.2	8.2	6.1	7.1
4	15.1	15.4	8.7	
5	11.5	5.9	13.4	6.9
6	8.0	4.9	9.1	6.0
7	2.7	3.0	6.9	6.0
8	4.6	8.4	—	8.2
9	—	8.6	9.1	10.5
10	9.5	3.4	4.7	12.3

Each year, numerous statistical services and business magazines will release annual reviews and surveys of sales, profits, and other figures, including returns on equity. One such survey conducted recently provided figures (which will change from one year to the next) for several selected industries. The table appears above.

Given the wide variety of returns, what constitutes an above-average return? There is no single answer, but in our super stock search we are looking for a company whose return is: (1) better than the competition; (2) above the aggregate rates of return of the companies in broad market averages such as the S&P and the Dow Industrials; and (3) above the prevailing level of interest rates. For the sake of this discussion, it can be said that any return on equity below 15 percent is not satisfactory. Moreover, like pretax margins, the *trend* is important. As the company gains maturity, its productivity improves and its assets are used to greater advantage.

Above-average returns fuel the ramjet engine of growth. If a company earns 20 percent on stockholders' equity and pays out half in dividends, the remaining 50 percent will be plowed back into the business to produce a future growth rate of roughly 10 percent; 20 percent × 50 percent. And if the company pays out only 15 percent of earnings as dividends, the remaining 85 percent, given a 20 percent rate of return on stockholders' equity, will sustain a growth rate of about 17 percent (20 percent × 85 percent)! In light of these calculations, a natural question becomes: Why doesn't management keep every last penny of earnings, paying out nothing? The answer to this question is considered later in the section: *Low, But Rising Dividends.*

RELATIVE EARNINGS PER SHARE GROWTH

Earnings can be increased in several ways: through cost reductions while sales remain relatively stable, thus improving profit margins; by increasing sales and maintaining the same profit margins; or, in the ideal situation, by increasing sales and increasing profit margins at the same time. Accordingly, a super stock is one that increases its sales at a fast clip while improving margins. But note that increased sales is a usual requirement for significant earnings growth. And note also that while total earnings are important, earnings per share is the key element watched by investors.

Any study of high-performance stocks reveals that their earnings increased at a compound annual rate in excess of both the Dow and the S&P. Stock prices react immediately to any significant change in either current earnings or short-term earnings prospects. In a sense, we're trying to buy *growing* earnings as cheaply as possible. This is related to three factors: the rate of future earnings growth of the company, the degree of certainty that this growth will occur, and the price earnings multiple.

Not all earnings are the same. A dollar of earnings by one company can be valued differently by investors than that same dollar generated by another company. The dependability of earnings could be one factor. The state of the economy and monetary conditions (particularly interest rates) could be another. They all affect investor psychology and thus the price earnings multiple. For example, the Dow Jones Industrial Average once sold at 23 times the earnings of its component stocks (in 1961) but it has also sold at 6 or 7 times those earnings in other years.

A good example of this phenomenon occurred in the heyday of growth stocks between 1960 and 1972. At this time, there was a mania among institutional investors for growing and predictable earnings. It was the period of what many called "the two-tiered market."

Mr. V.T. Norton, then Chairman for the Board of the Amerace Corporation, gave a dramatic example of the two-tiered market where large institutions where buying stocks of the *favorite fifty*. As the theory goes, they have superior growth in both earnings and dividends, which entitles them to high multiples.

Mr. Norton was in disagreement. According to him, "A substantial portion of these high multiples is caused by what has been labeled an 'inadvertent conspiracy' created when the institutions get on and ride. Having taken major positions for themselves or their clients, their continued recommendations or purchases of these stocks may well be in fact a conflict of interest."

Mr. Norton added that no one would "quarrel" with the premise that good continuous earnings should be attractive to investors. "Some companies," he said, "should enjoy higher price-earnings multiples than others. However, this does not justify the stratospheric multiples in the stocks that are the darlings of the money managers."

Mr. Norton then pointed out the earnings record of his company, Amerace, compared with one of the premier growth stocks of the period . . . one of the most favored of the favorite fifty:

Year	Amerace	Avon
1968	$2.00	$1.24
1969	1.77	1.47
1970	1.81	1.72
1971	2.14	2.16
Total share earnings (five years)	$9.69	8.48
Dividends (five years)	$6.00	$5.38

It is clear that Amerace earned more money per share than Avon during the period. The problem, of course, was that Amerace's earnings were neither growing nor consistent. The break in 1969 earnings posed a major question of continuity. The premium then, as now, was on consistency of earnings growth. At the time of Mr. Norton's comments, his company, Amerace, was selling at a price earnings ratio of 6 and Avon was selling at 50! Was Avon worth such a premium for consistency? In hindsight, the answer was no. Avon's stock later went from its multiple of 50 to a single digit multiple when earnings declined and investor psychology turned sour.

What determines price earnings multiples is the expected future rate of growth of a company's earnings and the stability of these future earnings. Once this stability (or persistency) has been established, the price that investors are willing to pay for that certainty goes up, as it did with Avon. But woe unto the company that, after compiling an excellent long-term growth rate, suddenly suffers a break in earnings.

This, of course, is what happened in the case of Avon and many others in the early 1970s.

Not too many years ago, a fairly exhaustive study was conducted to determine the answer to the question: What is the major factor that will determine the performance of a company's stock in the future (over the next 2 to 3 years). The approach involved gathering a universe of companies with similar fundamental and technical characteristics. This group consisted of all companies from 1966 to 1973 that showed each of the following three characteristics of April 30th of 1973:

1). a Price/Earnings Ratio of 40 or greater;
2). a market value of $100 million or higher;
3). most recently reported earnings at a maximum level for the prior five years.

There were 116 companies with these characteristics, including Avon, Baxter Labs, Corning Glass, Eastman Kodak, Johnson & Johnson, Eli Lilly, and so on. The second step was to note the earnings and price performance of these companies over the 3 years following.

Eighty-six of the 116 companies showed an earnings increase over the next 3 years while only 30 showed an earnings decrease. The average price change of these 116 companies over the subsequent 3 years was + 7%. Thus, over this period, these companies performed about in line with the market.

The major result, however, was that the 86 companies showing an earnings increase during this period actually performed very well indeed. They enjoyed an average price appreciation of 42 percent. About 3 out of 4 of these companies actually showed a rise in price, whereas only 1 out of 4 showed a decline.

The companies that showed an earnings decrease registered an average price decline of 60 percent. Only 1 out of 30 companies showing an earnings decline managed to show a price advance. Companies showing an earnings increase showed price appreciation more than 100 percent better than the companies showing an earnings decrease.

Eight of the ten companies that showed the largest earnings increase during this period went up in price and their average gain was 60.3 percent. The ten companies that showed the worst earnings performance declined an average of 58.4 percent in just three years. The latter group also included two companies that fell into bankruptcy.

In summary, this study indicated that the one factor that determined the price appreciation of all the large growth companies in this review was *earnings increases.*

Finally, the New York Stock Exchange monitors the high-earnings performers among its listed companies. In the more than 2 decades to 1980 in which statistics have been compiled on listed companies, only 12 have consistently, year in and year out, increased sales, net income and earnings per share. The next two tables present that select group arrayed two ways: first, size, and then earnings per share growth.

Can you guess which of these companies had the best stock performance in the same period? You guessed it! Baxter's stock rose by a fantastic 8,220 percent!

With this background, then, it's easy to see why "relative earnings growth" is an important factor in our search for the next super stock. One fast and easy way to make this calculation is to compare the earnings per share growth of our super stock candidates to the earnings growth of the "market" over some recent time frame. Because 1 year is a fairly short period of time, and much can happen to a small, rapidly growing company in 5 years, 3 years was selected for this study. Simply calculate the growth of earnings per share over the past 3 years. Then, compare it to the growth of the Dow Industrial's earnings (see Appendix B) over the same period. Thus, we have a means of judging relative earnings growth.

Company	1980 SALES (in millions)
1. Procter & Gamble	$10,772
2. Beatrice Foods	8,772
3. Philip Morris, Inc.	7,328
4. American Home Products	3,798
5. Bristol-Myers	3,158
6. Kellogg Co.	2,150
7. Petrolane, Inc.	1,425
8. Chesebrough-Ponds	1,377
9. Baxter Travenol Labs	1,374
10. Deluxe Check Printers	428
11. NCH	322
12. Jostens	295

Company	Earnings Per Share Growth 23-Yr. Annual Compound Rate
1. Baxter Travenol Labs	20.0%
2. NCH	18.6%
3. Deluxe Check Printers	17.3%
4. Petrolane, Inc.	17.2%
5. Jostens	16.1%
6. Philip Morris, Inc.	15.0%
7. Bristol-Myers	14.7%
8. Chesebrough-Ponds	12.6%
9. Kellogg Co.	10.5%
10. American Home Products	10.4%
11. Procter & Gamble	10.4%
12. Beatrice Foods	9.3%

LOW, BUT RISING DIVIDENDS

Dividends are clinically explained as the proportion of net earnings paid out to stockholders by a corporation. The dividend payment by a corporation is statistically portrayed in two ways: dividend yield and dividend payout. Like the price earnings ratio, dividend statistics are an important indicator of a company's value in the marketplace and its future growth. Dividend yield is expressed as a percentage calculated by dividing the current annual dividend by the market price of the stock. Since the price of a stock changes from day to day, so does the yield.

Yields are calculated daily for listed stocks in the stock tables of most major newspapers. Yields on over-the-counter stocks appear on a weekly basis in financial weeklies such as *Barron's*. The percentage of the company's earnings paid out in dividends to the stockholders is called the dividend payout ratio. If a company earns $1.00 per share and pays out $0.10 per share, the payout ratio is 10 percent.

A company with growing earnings has two choices: it can pay the earnings out in dividends, or it can keep the money in the company, plowing it back into the business to earn even more money. Both dividends and retained earnings have already been taxed once, but dividends will be taxed again once distributed to the shareholder. Retained earnings, on the other hand, can be reinvested in the business tax-free. If management is doing its job, it should be able to earn a greater return for shareholders than they can earn left to their own devices.

The dividend payout ratio is important because of the taxes on dividends and the tax-free nature of the plowback in earnings. If invested properly, this plowback increases earnings power, and eventually the price of the stock. Thus, we have a long-term capital gains potential. Long-term capital gains (assets held more than 1 year) are subject to taxation only upon sale of the appreciated asset and at rates less than at income tax rates. As a result, for most investors, after-tax dividend dollars are worth less than capital gains dollars. It also means that low-dividend-payout stocks of rapid-growth businesses are more attractive to investors in high tax brackets.

Interestingly, there is a prevailing view that a high payout gives the investor some protection in the event of a market decline. At some point in a stock's decline, the theory goes, the yield on a stock will be so high that the stock will be cushioned from going down any further. Unfortunately, this theory ignores the fact that concern over the future viability of earnings is one of the main reasons a stock declines in the first place. And once the future earnings stream comes into question, investors will usually give little credit to the current dividend. They realize if earnings fall, the dividend will soon follow and there goes the yield. There is, therefore, one rule worth noting: "If you have a choice between buying a stock that yields 2 percent and one that yields 7 percent, and have absolutely no other information at all about the two stocks, you can, without hesitation, select the stock yielding 2 percent. Nine times out of ten it will turn out to be the better investment of the two."

So, in general, low dividend payouts are better than high dividend payouts. And, if this is true, then no payout must be even better. Right? Logical, but incorrect as far as the stock market is concerned. For one thing, a great many institutions will not place a stock on their "buy" list unless it pays a dividend. A dividend makes the stock a true investment. Moreover, as the discussion in Chapter 4 demonstrated, dividends play an important role in an investor's portfolio.

Also important is the fact that a dividend, particularly a dividend rising over time, is often a "signal" from management to the investing public. Generally, changes in stock prices come about by changes in investor expectation about future earnings. Dividend increases indicate management's confidence that earnings increases will be forthcoming. That's a signal investors like because managements are usually extremely reluctant to increase dividends unless they're certain of future earnings gains.

Dividend decisions are based on management's desire to establish a pattern of stable dividend growth. A reluctance to change prevails both in regard to dividend increases and decreases. Increases in dividends are slow in coming because this indicates a commitment to continue paying at that level. A number of studies, some based on interviews with corporate management and others that have reviewed dividend histories, reaffirm the point that companies do not make dividend changes without considerable reflection about the future. Reductions usually occur only when companies have no other choice. Therefore, dividend changes reflect management's opinion about the future and should serve as indicators of a firm's future prosperity.

Clearly, from the investor's standpoint, the ideal dividend is a realistic balance between the company's needs for future growth and the investor's reward for patience.

What is the right balance? There is no definite answer, but consider the following table:

POTENTIAL ANNUAL GROWTH RATE

(Reinvestment Rate)

Return on Equity	Payout 0	10%	**20%**	**30%**	**40%**	**50%**
10%	10%	9%	8%	7%	6%	5%
15%	15%	14%	12%	11%	9%	8%
20%	20%	18%	16%	14%	12%	10%
25%	25%	23%	20%	18%	15%	13%
30%	30%	27%	24%	21%	18%	15%
35%	35%	32%	28%	25%	21%	18%
40%	40%	36%	32%	28%	24%	20%

Source: Based on the Reinvestment Rate formula as described in *Understanding Wall Street, 1982.* (Liberty Publishing Company, Inc.)

The table illustrates, for example, that if a company has a return on average stockholders' equity of 20 percent and a payout ratio of 30 percent (i.e., a plowback of 70 percent), the investor can expect an annual earnings growth rate of approximately 14 percent. The higher the ROE, the more a company can afford to pay in dividends without affecting earnings growth. If our super stock candidate has little hope for a return on equity of much more than 15 percent, a payout ratio of 40 percent is high enough!

LOW DEBT RATIO

Many investors swear they'll only invest in companies with "clean" balance sheets; that is, no debt. Unfortunately, these investors could be missing some good opportunities because debt, used properly, can increase earnings dramatically. Take the case of a corporation in the 1960s that sold bonds at a 5 percent interest rate. That's cheap capital today, and since interest costs are deductible, the after-tax cost to the company is even less. Using debt to increase earnings is called "leveraging," and many companies have been successful using this technique.

"The problem with debt is that it has to be paid off—usually at the most inconvenient time for a corporation . . . ." The speaker was one of the founding duPonts in a letter to a friend. This comment reflects DuPont Company's problem with debt in its formative years and explains the company's aversion to debt, at least until recent times.

An old rule of thumb says that debt is dangerous for cyclical companies, such as the steels and autos. In these cases, it was said, preferred stock should be substituted, and then a payment (the dividend) can be missed without financial disaster. This point ignores the obvious additional expense for safety: interest payments are deductible for tax purposes; preferred dividends are not. Where a corporation has a 50 percent effective tax rate, the cost of preferred financing, then, is twice that of bonds. Is safety worth the additional cost?

With leveraging, wide changes in earnings may be expected because debt interest payments and/or preferred-dividend-payments must be absorbed before anything is left for common stockholders. It works to the advantage of shareholders when earnings are good. It works against them when earnings are bad. Take the case of leverage at work with ABC Company. Over an economic cycle comprising a 5-year period, sales go up steadily through the first 3 years. Profit margins are maintained as sales increase, allowing earnings, before interest, to benefit directly from the increased revenues. Indeed, earnings rise dramatically from $0.24 a share to $0.39. But as the recession hits in the fourth year, the decline is dramatic.

The wide swing in earnings is accentuated by the subtraction of the fixed amount of interest expense. In other words, the excess of

		—Years—			
	1	2	3	4	5
Earnings Before Interest	$580,000	$720,000	$870,000	$280,000	$ 30,000
Interest Expense	100,000	100,000	100,000	100,000	100,000
Earnings Before Income Taxes	480,000	620,000	770,000	180,000	(70,000)
Income Taxes (@ 50%)	240,000	320,000	385,000	90,000	—
Net Earnings	240,000	320,000	385,000	90,000	(70,000)
Net Earnings Per Share	.24	.32	.39	.09	(.07)

the rate earned on investment over the rate paid for borrowed money is the degree of leverage. In this example, the fifth year is critical; total earnings are not enough to cover the interest payments and ABC company has to dip into reserves to pay the interest. If there are no reserves to make the interest payments, or if the debt is close to maturity, the company could be in deep trouble—financial insolvency at worst, and financial embarrassment at best. Leverage, then, works both ways. It magnifies the good times and bad times alike. Accordingly, a shift in the company's cost structure toward more fixed costs of any type (debt, of course, is not the only kind) tends to increase the magnitude of investment risk.

Given the dangers of too much debt, is there a rule that investors can follow? The answer depends on the industry and stability of earning power, the company's profitability (especially measured by the return on shareholders' equity), and, of course, the level of interest rates (a 20 percent interest rate can be a much greater drain on the company's resources than, say, a rate of 4 percent). For utilities, where the markets are monopolistic with only one company in the area, a debt level of 50 or 60 percent of the total capitalization is not out of line. For cyclical companies such as steel, aluminum, and copper companies, debt percentages above 25 percent of total capitalization should be viewed very carefully. With growth companies, we can be somewhat more liberal. Our rule should be that debt will not exceed 35 percent of the total capitalization. This means that, roughly, debt should not be more than 50 percent of stockholders' equity—especially if the return on stockholders' equity is less than 20 percent. When interest rates are high, the lower the debt, the better.

Year	Sales ($mm)	— Per Share — Earnings	Dividend
1980	$709.6	$0.76	$0.10
1979	648.8	0.92	—
1978	575.6	0.94	—
1977	511.5	0.59	—
1976	474.7	0.53	—

1980 Capitalization

Debt	$210.0 million
Equity	127.8 million

7,100,000 shares outstanding

Could this company be in trouble? Management appears optimistic. The company declared a cash dividend for the first time in nearly 20 years and the stock is listed on the New York Stock Exchange. That's right! This company, Saxon Industries, declared bankruptcy in 1982. A quick glance at the figures, of course, tells the investor that Saxon was never close to being a super stock (note, for example, the low profit margins and the poor return on stockholders' equity). However, this example does show what can happen when debt is too high, even though sales are increasing and the company is profitable.

INSTITUTIONAL HOLDINGS

Investors are always surprised when they discover a company that has earnings per share growth well above average over a considerable period of time and yet its stock has not advanced substantially in price. Suspiciously, they begin to believe something must be wrong. And yet further checking produces no flaws: unit sales volume up, pretax profit margins up, the return on equity up. All the characteristics of a super stock exist, and still the price has failed to keep pace with these achievements. The primary reason, of course, is *size*. The company is simply too small for institutions to buy the stock in a big way.

Most big institutions are interested only in companies with capitalizations above $200 million and only a few will buy when a capitalization is much under $50 million. This is where the flexibility and patience of the individual investor can become a substantial advantage.

You can find the institutional ownership of most companies in Vickers or from Moody's or Standard & Poor's. The Standard & Poor's monthly stock guide, for example, lists more than 5300 common and preferred stocks with some operating history, financial statistics, etc. One of the columns lists the number of institutions holding the stock and the number of shares owned. The data covers almost 2700 institutions including investment companies, banks, insurance companies, college endowments, and so on.

We want our stock to be relatively unknown—but not completely. Some modest institutional ownership is comforting. Institutions spend a lot of time and money researching a stock. Their research is intensive and thorough and most investors know it. So, having a few institutions own the stock represents respectability and a vindication of our research process. It also suggests that other investors with more sophisticated tools and resources independently agree regarding our target company's growth and prospect. It's almost a badge of acceptance. But just as with dividends, a little ownership is fine, but not too much.

The company is still to be "discovered" when institutional ownership is below 10 percent. Usually, by the time holdings exceed 15 percent, the stock is on the "approved lists" of a large number of institutions. Dave Baker, one of the most successful and respected portfolio managers on Wall Street once said: "When all the institutions are in . . . there's no one else with big buying power to put the stock price up further. Success is only greeted with a yawn . . . it's expected. But failure . . . a bad quarter . . . and all the institutions will want to go out of the door at once. It can make for a very volatile stock . . . and a disappointing one."

In 2 or 3 years, perhaps, our super stock's high rate of growth in sales and earnings will begin to place it on the edge of consideration among the smaller institutions. They will begin to buy and put the price up. The company's rapid growth will raise earnings per share and, with it, increased institutional acceptance will expand the multiple. Since capitalization requirements of an institution is a function of both shares outstanding and price, growth in earnings, coupled with the higher multiple, will ultimately place our selected stock within the universe of most institutions. And institutions will be important in our stock's future; for it is *they who will contribute much of that second ingredient to our "Magic Combination," thus making it a "super" stock.*

PRICE-EARNINGS MULTIPLE

A basic tool in valuing earnings is the price earnings multiple, or P/E ratio. This indicates what the stock market is willing to pay for a dollar of earnings. Price earnings multiples are important since appreciation in a growth stock is achieved not only by the steadily increasing per-share earnings, but also through a rising P/E ratio. This point is best shown by this example of an 8-year price appreciation of American Home Products Corporation from 1953 through 1961:

Year	Sales	Earnings Per Share	Year End Market Price	P/E Ratio
1961	$468.2 mm	$2.16	$78	36.1x
1960	446.5	2.09	60	28.7
1959	420.8	2.02	58	28.7
1958	374.9	1.84	43	23.4
1957	347.2	1.68	26	15.5
1956	295.5	1.36	21	15.4
1955	234.5	0.89	15	16.9
1954	203.1	0.70	11	15.7
1953	188.3	0.57	8	14.0

It should be noted that the preceding figures are somewhat exaggerated because P/E multiples of most stocks were expanding during this period, but not quite to this extent. (See Appendix B). Between 1953 and 1961, American Home's stock advanced 875 percent. Without *any* multiple expansion, the advance would have been "only" 278 percent.

But a stock's P/E ratio is more than just a relationship of the current price to annual earnings. It is a thermometer of investor attitudes toward a particular stock within the context of its environment. These attitudes encompass future earnings growth and the certainty of those earnings. Further, one can, and should, compare this thermometer reading to the price earnings ratio of the overall market. Either the Dow Jones Industrial Average (Appendix B) or Standard & Poor's are commonly used as comparative indices. The "market" price earnings ratio reflects the sum of all investors' attitudes on the future, including the outlook for the economy, as well as returns on competing investments. And the market will generally pay more when alternative investments are less attractive. For this reason, investors watch the level of interest rates. When interest rates are high, P/E multiples tend to be low and vice versa. The ratio also varies among industries, and even within a single industry. Usually, more will be paid for a dollar of earnings in a bull market than in a bear market (sometimes enthusiasm feeds upon itself). Further, more will be paid for a dollar of rising earnings than for declining earnings.

"The stock market looks cheap!" How often have you heard this comment? In this instance, the "market" is the Dow Jones Industrial Average. "Cheap" refers to what you have to pay to buy current earnings. But how cheap is cheap? Consider the wide swing in the Dow Average: 7 times earnings in 1949 to 23 times in 1961. Was 7 cheap? Not necessarily. Actually the Dow in this century has sold as low as 3.8 times earnings in 1917 (in this case, based on the mean price for each year) and as high as 38 times earnings in 1933. The year 1933 was in the depths of the depression. Why was the P/E so high? Because the price earnings multiple anticipated better times ahead when earnings were at or near their lowest point. In 1933, the market was close to its lowest level. On the same basis, then, the lowest multiples of earnings are sometimes recorded when investors regard those earnings as peak earnings. They're saying that earnings might not be going higher and they don't want to pay much for peak earnings.

Twenty years ago, the P/E multiple of the Dow Industrials was near 20 times earnings, which tells us that investors were quite optimistic about the future—certainly more so than they have been in recent years.

Sometimes price earnings multiples don't matter. Most "asset plays," such as oil and gas exploration companies or mining companies, frequently sell at extremely high price/earnings multiples, despite often erratic earnings records. These companies tend to be valued on the basis of reserves in the ground and "cash flow" (earnings plus all noncash expenses such as depreciation and depletion) rather than earnings. However, for most industrial stocks, analysts tend to compare a company's earnings and dividend prospects with that of the overall market to determine whether it is undervalued.

Further, the P/E of the target stock can be compared to other stocks in its industry. For example, if Digital Equipment were selling at 18 times earnings, IBM at 12 times earnings, and the Dow Industrials at 9, then Digital is being valued at 50 percent more than IBM and twice the "market." This is a quantitative evaluation of investor views about earnings growth rates.

In the early 1970s, most money managers were eagerly buying growth stocks. The idea was that persistent earnings growth of 10 to 15 percent was worth a high multiple and that there was less risk in buying a growth stock selling at 35 times earnings and risking a decline to 25 earning times than buying a cyclical stock at 12 times peak earnings that could eventually go to six times depressed earnings. As it turned out, this thesis was irresistible to the big banks (particularly those in New York City) and money managers were buying proven growth stocks like Avon, IBM, Xerox, etc.

Eventually, the list of "provens" was narrowed down to about fifty stocks, the so-called "nifty fifty." "Growth" they said, "would never go out of style." Buying for growth meant that these money managers could avoid income stocks, or acquisition candidates, or cyclical turnarounds. All they had to do was concentrate on the big growth companies and pour tens of millions of dollars into the market. What they didn't realize was that, while growth would not go out of style, you could pay too much for growth. The inevitable result: when earnings faltered, stock prices crashed!

Now the reverse is true. Excessive government spending, inflation, and high interest rates have taken their toll on P/E multiples since the 1960s. While it has been a difficult investment environment in recent years, particularly after the market crash in the fall of 1987, it could also be a major benefit to buyers of super stocks in the years immediately ahead.

THE SCORECARD

Ultimately, the real mark of a super stock is a strong and persistent demand for the company's products and services. The Super Stock Scorecard is not a predictive device, but rather a reliable screen of nine specific categories that have been reviewed carefully. This screen merely tells us that the company is well positioned to meet that demand and to return a good profit to the stockholders. Each of these categories was found common to most super stocks of the past. Collectively, they are only a starting point for further analysis. The long-term picture and the company's fundamentals need to be examined with care. And, more times than not, an investor can anticipate a company's success by plain 'ole common sense.

Of these categories listed, seven are assigned "points." A score of 80 points or more tells us this investment has the characteristics of a future super stock. Less than 80 suggests that the company be reviewed again later, or that the stock be dropped altogether.

Thus far, all of these categories have been described in some detail. Now, let's construct the scorecard for your future stock selections.

☑ Size

There are no points assigned to this category. However, a company with sales between $25 million and $500 million should be given priority.

☑ Unit Sales Volume(Max. 15 Points)

Assign 15 points to the scorecard if, over the past 3 years, sales increased by a greater amount (total percent) than did CPI in the same period. (See Appendix A). If applicable, adjust prior years for acquisitions. For each year CPI outpaced sales growth within the past three years, deduct 5 points.

☑ Pretax Profit Margin (Max. 15 Points)

A rising trend in pretax margins over the past 5 to 10 years is awarded 10 points. Add 5 points if the pretax margin currently is above 10%. Deduct 3 points for each year (within the past 3 years) that the pretax margin declined from the preceding year.

☑ Return on Stockholders' Equity (Max. 30 Points)

In your judgement, does the company (within the next 2 years) have the potential for an annual return of at least 15% on average stockholders' equity? If the answer to this question is "no," rate this category "zero points" and proceed to another investment opportunity. If so, add 25 points to the scorecard. Add another 5 points if ROE is *currently* above 15%. Deduct 10 points if ROE is not in a rising trend (over the past 5 to 10 years), taking into account the possibility that recent figures may have been unduly depressed by an economic recession.

☑ **Relative Earnings Per Share Growth (Max. 20 Points)**

If, over the past 3 years, the company's earnings per share advanced by a larger percentage increase than that calculated for per-share earnings of the Dow Industrials, add 20 points. Any adjustments or allowances for extraordinary events that may have disrupted the company's normal performance during this period should be made with care. Many companies report "nonrecurring" problems regularly.

☑ **Dividends (Max. 5 Points)**

No points are awarded to a company that does not pay a dividend or if the dividend trend over the past 5 years is not rising. If the dividend is in a rising trend and the payout ratio is below 40%, add 5 points. If the payout ratio is above 40%, the 5 points are not awarded *unless* the Earned Growth Rate is above 7.5%.

☑ **Debt Structure (Max. 10 Points)**

If the company's long-term debt is below 35% of stockholders' equity, add 10 points. Add only 5 points if long-term debt is above 35% (but less than 50%) of stockholders' equity. Do not award any points if long-term debt is more than 50% of stockholders' equity. If debt exceeds stockholders' equity, *deduct* 10 points.

☑ **Institutional Holdings (Max. 5 Points)**

Assign 5 points to the scorecard if institutions do not own more than 10% of the outstanding shares. If more than 10% (but less than 15%) is held, add only 2 points. Do not award any points if institutional ownership exceeds 15% of the outstanding shares.

☑ **Price Earnings Multiple**

While there are no points assigned to this category, super stocks will, by definition, outperform the overall market over the long term. It is not unusual for a super stock to temporarily underperform other stocks in a bear market. However, if the stock has not been advancing at least as well as the Dow Jones Industrial Average in a favorable market environment, beware! This factor can be a useful confirmation of your analytical work.

6

The Search Begins

FINANCIAL PRACTICE WITHOUT THE EMOTIONAL EXPERIENCE OF IN-vesting has been regarded by cynics as impractical. One answer to the cynics is to point to the success of major graduate business schools such as Harvard, Stanford, and Columbia who train managers for industry through "practice." In other words, by analyzing and solving actual business cases, in time, the student's skills are polished to a high degree without the pain or expense of industry apprenticeship. Similarly, we can profit by analyzing some actual "cases"—statistical profiles of companies to fine tune our ability to uncover a super stock. As these cases demonstrate, in the real world, some judgement is needed. Unfortunately, stock selection is still an art as much as it is a science.

CASE 1: ALPHA CORPORATION

Our first case study is a company we'll call Alpha Corporation, in the initial stages of marketing a new product that seemed to be a technological marvel of sophistication and great utility.

It's the first quarter of 1960. By leafing through the over-the-counter stock reports or reading the Wall Street Journal, one would have been impressed by the 1959 earnings report of Alpha: sales up 15 percent; earnings per share up more than 22 percent. A quick look at the stock's price record indicated that it had gradually been advancing. Finally, another good sign, a 4 for 1 stock split had been effected in December, 1959. Further investigation is definitely warranted.

Financial references such as *Standard & Poor's, Moody's,* or *Barron's* would have provided the sales and earnings record over the past 9 years as follows:

	Total Revenues	Net Income Per Share
1959	$31,739	$.60
1958	27,576	.49
1957	25,807	.46
1956	23,560	.40
1955	21,390	.38
1954	17,318	.27
1953	15,751	.20
1952	14,755	.19
1951	12,897	.16

Alpha's record over the years has fulfilled initial expectations. Seeing statistics of this type makes the drudgery of financial investigation worthwhile.

Knowing that a new product or process can create substantial increases in earnings, the serious searcher may have sifted through an average of a dozen companies each month that initially appeared to have interesting possibilities. A brief investigation of the past 5-or 10-year record would usually show a start-and-stumble sales and earnings record: up and then down, or flat, for several years, then up again. Erratic operating figures would probably be our first reason for elimination of a stock from our list. In this case, Alpha's growth has been not just steady, but accelerating. Alpha's 1958 performance was especially impressive when compared to other companies at that time.

Size, too, is a common rejection factor. Many companies with sales over a half billion dollars, particularly in the late 1950s, would be culled from the list. This is not to say that large, older companies cannot grow, too. Occasionally, they do. In fact, during this time frame of 1950 to

1960, one old-line large company did do well: DuPont. DuPont was *the* chemical producer and from 1953 to 1955 its earnings and future prospects looked extremely attractive. An investment in DuPont in 1953 tripled by 1955. But that was unusual. During this same period most of the big chemical, steel, aluminum, and auto manufacturers were poor investments. However, Alpha's record is different and the company's size in terms of sales is about right. The growth trend is strong: sales up 146 percent and earnings per share up 275 percent. That's the type of fast-track growth we want. But will further research disappoint us? You be the judge. The statistics that were available back in early 1960 are presented on the next page.

As noted earlier, the company's current sales rate (in 1959) suggests the proper size range: large enough to grow and finance itself, but not so large that it has the built-in drag of large numbers.

A review of a more detailed financial statement such as Alpha's annual report or a Standard & Poor's or Moody's analysis sheet indicates that sales during the 1950s have been rising faster than the current rate of inflation; as measured by the Consumer Price Index. (Also, see Appendix A). In the 10 years covered, not only have dollar sales gone up, but unit sales volume has also increased. Further, it is worth noting that sales have included a small but growing portion of equipment rentals and royalties that are more stable revenues.

The pretax profit margins can be calculated from the data by dividing the pretax income by sales as follows:

	Sales, etc.	Pretax Income	Pretax Profit Margins
1959	$31,739	$4,681	14.7%
1958	27,576	3,734	13.5
1957	25,807	3,399	13.2
1956	23,560	2,936	12.5
1955	21,390	2,642	12.4
1954	17,318	2,079	12.0
1953	15,751	1,685	10.7
1952	14,755	1,509	10.2
1951	12,897	1,088	8.4
1950	10,027	1,048	10.5

ALPHA CORPORATION SELECTED FINANCIAL DATA
(Thousands of Dollars)

	1959	1958	1957	1956	1955	1954	1953	1952	1951	1950
Sales/Gross Revenues	$31,739	$27,576	$25,807	$23,560	$21,390	$17,318	$15,751	$14,755	$12,897	$10,027
Pre-tax Income	4,681	3,734	3,399	2,936	2,642	2,079	1,685	1,509	1,088	1,048
Income Tax	2,600	2,107	1,905	1,634	1,480	1,195	1,135	1,009	687	548
Net Income	2,081	1,627	1,494	1,302	1,162	884	550	500	401	500
Dividends (Common)	793	658	645	637	450	400	370	321	302	299
Long Term Debt	4,800	2,900	3,000	3,002	3,008	3,013	768	873	977	—
Stockholders' Equity	17,615	14,715	12,600	11,056	7,959	7,246	6,773	6,593	5,096	4,873
Common Shares Outstanding (Thousands)	3,460	3,309	3,265	3,225	3,085	3,085	2,265	2,265	2,265	2,265
Per Share ($)										
Net Income	.60	.49	.46	.40	.38	.27	.20	.19	.16	.20
Dividends	.21¼	.20	.20	.20	.14½	.13	.12	.12	.12	.12

The tabulation is eloquent enough: Alpha's margins are in a rising trend. Note the steady increase over the years and the strong showing in 1958, a recession year.

Of all the measurements we are likely to use, the *return on stockholders' equity* calculation is the most important. Stockholders' equity is the total of the common stock account and retained earnings (net earnings less dividends). Another way to calculate stockholders' equity would be to deduct total liabilities from total assets—what's left belongs to the stockholders and can be defined as stockholders' equity. The return on stockholders' equity is computed by dividing the net earnings by the stockholders' equity figure. For example, the return on equity for the year 1959 developed as follows:

$$\frac{\text{Net income (1959)}}{\text{Stockholders' Equity (1959)}} = \frac{\$2,081}{17,615} = 11.8\%$$

These figures are not entirely accurate, however, because we are using total company income earned during the entire year, but only a year-end equity figure. It would be more accurate to use an *average* equity figure, obtained by averaging the year-beginning and the year-ending stockholders' equity totals. However, we're mostly interested in the long-term *trend* and *potential*. In this regard, the companies we definitely want to avoid are those that could *never*, even under optimistic circumstances, enjoy a return on equity of 15 percent or more. For this screening purpose, year-end figures are satisfactory. But once we examine the company more closely, we want to be more precise:

	Net Income	Average Stockholders' Equity	Average Return on Equity
1959	$2,081	$16,165	12.9%
1958	1,627	13,658	11.9%
1957	1,494	11,828	12.6%
1956	1,302	9,508	13.7%
1955	1,162	7,609	15.3%
1954	884	7,010	12.6%
1953	550	6,683	8.2%
1952	500	5,845	8.6%
1951	401	4,985	8.0%

Again, the test is passed with flying colors. During the decade of the 1950s, Alpha increased average stockholders' equity to more than three times what it was in 1951. At the same time, net income advanced to five times! Some judgment is involved, however. Investors in 1958 might have wondered, for example, whether a "new trend" had set in after 3 years of declining returns. But in long-term perspective, Alpha's return on equity was well maintained in the recession year 1958 when compared with the early 1950s. In addition, investors also knew by this time that a 15 percent return was not out of the question.

A return of 10 to 12 percent on equity during the decade of the 1950s was well above average; not only for Alpha's business but also compared with the overall return on equity in American industry. To determine what constitutes an above-average rate of return, we must compare the company's return against those of its competitors and against overall corporate results during the period measured.

How did Alpha's per-share earnings growth compare to the per-share-earnings growth of other stocks over the past few years? Here is a fast way to see:

	Alpha's EPS	Dow Industrial Average EPS*
1959	$0.60	$34.31
1956	0.40	33.34
% Change	+ 50%	+ 3%

*see Appendix "B"

In other words, by comparing the most recent earnings with the earnings of 3 years earlier, it is obvious that Alpha's progress has occurred *despite* the environment.

The dividend criterion is relatively easy to develop. Essentially, we want a company whose dividend policy is one of sharing some of its annually generated cash profits with the owners (shareholders). However, with a company that's effectively managed and positioned in a growing business, there are always innumerable profit opportunities that require money. Accordingly, as long as these opportunities exist, the company should be retaining its profits to invest for more profits. This means a low-dividend payout as a percentage of net income. In Alpha's case, the percentage is developed by dividing net income into annual dividends to determine the payout percentage as follows:

	Net Income	Dividends	Percent Payout
1959	$2,081	$793	38.1%
1958	1,627	658	40.4%
1957	1,494	645	43.2%
1956	1,302	637	48.9%
1955	1,162	450	38.7%
1954	884	400	45.2%
1953	550	370	67.3%
1952	500	321	64.2%
1951	401	302	75.3%
1950	500	299	59.8%
	+316%	+165%	

The resulting figures are somewhat surprising for a growth stock. The dividend payout was initially high—60 to 75 percent of earnings for several years before gradually falling back to below a 40 percent payout. We would prefer less payout and more plowback, as is usually the case with fast-growing companies. Nevertheless, the payout is not too high and dividends are rising. Overall, dividends paid increased each year in the 10-year period. This important factor will attract both individual and institutional investors.

The test for a moderate to low debt structure depends not so much on total debt, but on the relationship of debt to the company's financial structure. Of greatest concern would be long-term debt as it relates to the capital structure. In most companies, short-term debt is more than offset by current assets: cash and equivalents, account receivables, and inventories.

Within the production cycle, short-term debt is usually incurred to finance inventories of material needed to produce the product or service. After these inventories go through the production process and result in products or services that are shipped or billed, they become accounts receivable. Thus, while our current debt remains the same, inventories have been reduced and accounts receivable increased. After a 30- to 40-day billing cycle, the accounts receivable are paid off by the company's customers. The cash is used to pay off or reduce the current debt. Our focus, as investors, is on long-term debt since this is not self-liquidating, but depends on profits over time.

Long-term debt is usually expressed as a percent of total assets. But this measurement is too broad. Total assets include current as well as fixed assets and might be misleading since the type and quality of assets are not quantified. One other measure is more to the point: long-term debt as a percent of stockholders' equity. Less than 35 percent is comfortable. Above 100 percent (1 to 1) is considered high when the return on equity is less than 20 to 25 percent. In this case, the percentages develop as follows:

	Long Term Debt as % of Stockholders' Equity
1959	27.2%
1958	19.7%
1957	23.8%
1956	27.2%
1955	37.8%
1954	41.6%
1953	11.3%
1952	13.2%
1951	19.2%

Our next test of a super stock is the level of institutional holdings. How many institutions were interested in Alpha Corporation in 1960? Not many. As a matter of fact, except for one university and a few local banks, there was only minimal interest. All to the good. A few astute investing groups have discovered what we did, but not many. That leaves room for a substantial price move once large institutions become interested. Institutional holdings are listed in Standard & Poor's and in Vickers.

There is no better gauge of increasing investor enthusiasm for the company than a rising trend in the price they are willing to pay for a dollar of earnings; that is, the price earnings multiple. First consider the years 1950 through 1953. They were war years—the Korean Conflict. Investor attitudes were affected by the tug of two psychological factors: a widening of the war and wage/price controls. Accordingly, multiples meant little until after the Armistice in the summer of 1953. This was succeeded by a slowdown of the national economy from the summer of 1953 through 1954. It is more relevant, then, to measure investor attitudes in terms of multiples for 1955 through 1959, a normal 4 years of a peacetime economy.

	Earnings Per Share	Price Per Share High/Low	Price Earnings Ratio High/Low
1959	$ .60	$36 1/2 - 21 1/4	60.8 - 35.4
1958	.49	24 1/4 - 11 7/8	49.5 - 24.2
1957	.46	15 3/8 - 9	33.4 - 19.6
1956	.40	18 3/8 - 11	45.9 - 27.5
1955	.38	16 3/4 - 7 3/4	44.1 - 20.4

Here we see a gently rising price earnings ratio—nothing spectacular, but an indication that the investing community is paying increasing attention the company's operating performance. Is the price earnings ratio too high? We don't know. The Dow Jones Industrial Average was selling at about 20 times lacklustre earnings in early 1960. So, with Alpha's stock at $32, the multiple accorded these growing earnings did not seem out of line.

The trend of a rising P/E multiple cannot, of course continue forever. Stocks do go down from time to time. For this reason, we are concerned with Alpha's performance both compared with *itself* and compared with the *market* as a whole. We note that Alpha's average P/E increased from 32.3 in 1955 to 48.1 in 1959. In the same period, the Dow multiple increased from 12.3 to 18.3 times. Both advanced about 49 percent. However, Alpha's earnings were *up* while the earnings of the Dow Average *declined!* This not only speaks favorably for Alpha's fundamentals, but for its investment merit as well. It simply would have been more profitable to own Alpha than to own the Dow Industrials in this period.

In summary, let's review our analysis:

- *Size:* Nearly $32 million in sales—a small but growing company. The right size.

- *Unit Sales Volume:* Rising; up 28.4% over CPI since 1956 without a "negative" year. (15 points)

- *Pretax Profit Margins:* Above 10%; upward trend, rising every year over the past 8 years. Full point score. (15 points)

- *Return on Stockholders' Equity*: Above-average returns and rising. Capable of achieving at least 15%. (25 points)

- *Relative Earnings Per Share Growth:* Substantially better than the DJIA over the past three years (+ 50% vs DJIA + 3 %). (20 points)

- *Dividends:* A rising dividend trend and a current payout ratio that will allow for a plowback of earnings. (5 points)

- *Debt Structure:* Long term debt is not too high in relation to stockholders' equity. In 1959, debt was 27% of stockholders' equity. (10 points)

- *Institutional Holdings:* Low. (5 points)

- *Price Earnings Ratio:* Upward trend in line with the market.

According to our criteria, Alpha Corporation, with a total of 95 points, has all the ingredients of a super stock. But can we be sure? Should we wait and see evidence of a more vigorous earnings trend? The more we wait for verification, the higher the price we'll have to pay. But let's say we wanted to be sure and we waited another year. Now it's early 1961 and the trend continues but at an increased pace with sales of $37 million up 17 percent over 1959, net income of $2,598,329, up 25 percent over the prior year, and the stock price is approaching $100 per share, a triple in the price.

In actuality, Alpha Corporation is Haloid Xerox, now called Xerox Corporation. Although it was incorporated more than 50 years earlier, it did not break into super stock status until 1959 or 1960. The company, in 1959, was about to introduce its new Model 914, which marked the beginning of a revolution in office copiers. But you didn't have to know this—at least not initially—to recognize the stock's potential.

In reality in 1960, however, without knowing that Haloid Xerox equipment being shipped was *rented* and not *sold*, an investor looking only at the numbers could have been temporarily misled. The earnings benefits (and the return on equity) for the equipment being shipped to the field were not realized immediately. Actually, the company's return on equity declined in 1960 and did not begin its sharp ascent until 1961 (17.1 percent that year): 33.4 percent in 1962; 34.3 percent in 1963; and 36.4 percent in 1964! For this reason, it is important to judge a company's performance, not just on a year-to-year basis, but with a longer term perspective.

The rest, of course, is stock market history. By 1965, sales had multiplied more than tenfold, in only 5 years, to an incredible $392 million! Net income was $58.6 million! By the end of the 1960s, sales passed the billion dollar mark! Here are some of the appreciation percentages:

- For the very patient, the rewards were—as Dr. Samuel Johnson once said—beyond the dreams of avarice. A purchase of 100 shares of Haloid Xerox in 1958 for $4,750, a year before our discovery, became 6,000 shares in 1972 worth $1,031,250!

- In one year—1963—you could have bought Xerox in the first week of the year at a price of $150 to $160 and in the last week of the year sold it for $435, an increase of 180 percent in 12 months! In the next 8 years, the stock more than quintupled again!

Indeed, there were many plumbers, taxi drivers, and housewives in Rochester, New York who held onto their Xerox stock. They are now (and have been for a while) millionaires!

These results are eloquent testimony to the rewards of finding a super stock!

CASE 2: BETA CORPORATION

Our second case study, called Beta Corporation, may or may not be a super stock. That is for you to decide. Presented is a brief description of the company and its operations and selected array of statistics. A worksheet has been provided for us to use in calculating the company's qualifications.

Beta Corporation's business can be characterized as a growth area relying heavily on innovative products that appeal to the consumer. Basically, the business can be called entertainment and its growth and profitability depends on consumer disposable income.

The time frame has been moved forward several years to 1966. This was a period of the Great Society of President Lyndon Johnson and one of two wars; one on poverty and another in Vietnam. Inflation was low (but beginning to climb) and highgrade, long-term bonds were being sold at the then unbelievably high interest rate of 6 percent.

Our constant review of the financial section of newspapers gives us an idea of significant corporate operating results both quarterly and

BETA CORPORATION SELECTED FINANCIAL DATA
(Thousands of Dollars)

	1965	1964	1963	1962	1961	1960	1959	1958	1957	1956
Sales/Gross Revenues	$109,947	$86,651	$81,922	$75,612	$70,248	$50,931	$58,432	$48,577	$35,778	$27,565
Pre-tax Income	21,529	12,749	12,674	10,914	9,788	(2,642)	7,300	7,790	7,499	4,464
Income Tax	10,150	5,692	6,100	5,650	5,322	(1,300)	3,900	3,925	3,850	1,841
Net Income	11,379	7,057	6,574	5,264	4,466	(1,342)	3,400	3,865	3,649	2,623
Dividends (Common)	738	707	685	665	650	648	608	615	299	—
Long Term Debt	8,851	9,451	11,798	15,505	15,360	20,397	6,266	6,591	2,373	593
Stockholders' Equity	53,125	41,494	34,998	29,024	24,425	20,610	24,398	22,205	18,982	16,359
Common Shares Outstanding (Thousands)	1,870	1,838	1,833	1,830	1,830	1,830	1,833	1,890	1,890	1,654
Per Share ($)										
Net Income	6.08	3.83	3.59	2.88	2.44	(.73)	1.86	2.04	1.93	1.59
Dividends	0.39	0.38	0.37	0.36	0.36	0.36	0.33	0.33	0.16	—

annually. One day we come across the results of the Beta Corporation
for the latest September fiscal year as follows:

"Beta Corporation announced net profits after taxes for the
fiscal year (52 weeks) ended October 2, 1965 of
$11,378.778. representing $6.08 per share on the 1,870,097
shares outstanding at the fiscal year end. This compares
with last year's (53 weeks) net profit of $7,057,435 equal
to $3.83 per share on the 1,837,942 shares then outstanding
. . . gross revenues reached a record high totaling
$109,947,068, an increase of $23,295,960 . . ."

Beta Corporation is reporting astounding fiscal results. Gross
revenues increased more than 26 percent, but net income increased
more than 61 percent. Beta Corporation is well worth further
investigation. But come to your own conclusion. In this case study,
and in the others that follow, you will be given a 10-year summary
of all the statistics needed to make the necessary calculations. Follow
the same line of reasoning used in the Haloid Xerox example and fill
out the "scorecard."

	Beta P/E Ratio		Dow Industrials P/E	
	High	*Low*	*High*	*Low*
Early 1966	Approximately 9.6x		Approximately 17.0x	
1965	10.3	6.4	18.1	15.7
1964	12.9	9.6	19.2	16.5
1963	12.2	7.2	18.6	15.7

Additional facts that were not in the financials but could have been
researched, are given as follows:

Institutional holdings: According to a 1966 Standard & Poor's *Stock
Guide*, 17 institutions hold 134,000 shares, or about 7 percent of the
1.9 million total shares outstanding.

Almost from the outset in 1966, Beta's stock price as well as most
other stocks, seemed to be in a steady decline. However, Beta was
clearly outperforming the market. At the end of April, 1966, the stock
was still well above its lows of the fourth quarter of 1965; the Dow
Industrials had fallen much further.

```
┌────────────── BETA CORPORATION ──────────────┐
│                SUPER STOCK SCORECARD          │
```

BETA CORPORATION
SUPER STOCK SCORECARD

Score

☐ Size* .... (Confirm)

☐ Unit Sales Volume.......................

☐ Pretax Profit Margins....................

☐ Return on Stockholders' Equity............

☐ Relative Earnings Per Share Growth........

☐ Dividends...............................

☐ Debt Structure...........................

☐ Institutional Holdings....................

☐ Price Earnings Ratio*.................... (Confirm)

Total

*No score necessary

With the calculations and scorecard completed, let's analyze the results. Beta has nearly $110 million in sales, more than three times the sales size of Haloid Xerox when it first appeared in our financial readings. Larger, indeed, but well within our range of interest.

Sales volume has been in a significant uptrend over the 10-year period. Again, while it's difficult to equate dollar volume with unit volume, our basic standard is that sales volume increases should not be solely the result of price increases due to inflation. Checking the Consumer Price Index in Appendix A would verify that the year-to-year sales increase, especially in the past 3 years, were well ahead of the year-to-year increases in the CPI. Sales advanced from $75,612,000 in 1962 to nearly $110,000,000 in 1965, an increase of 45 percent while the CPI in the same period rose only about 5 percent.

Pretax profit margins (net income before taxes, divided by sales or, in this case, gross revenues) are healthy and have been rising—another plus for super stock status. However, we note that 1960 was unprofitable and that margins declined in 1964.

Management's efficiency in generating an attractive return on the stockholders' investment is also well demonstrated in this 10-year period. Return on stockholders' equity (net income after taxes divided by stockholders' equity) has been in an uptrend and well above 15 percent. However, the year 1960 deserves further investigation. When related to the rate of return earned on stockholders' equity for other corporations during the comparable period, this company's return is especially noteworthy. In 1965, the Earned Growth Rate was more than 25 percent!

In the past 3 years, Beta's earnings advanced from $2.98 to $6.08 per share, an increase of 111 percent. This growth compares to a 47 percent increase for the Dow Jones Industrials—from $36.43 in 1962 to $53.67 in 1965. This is certainly a positive sign.

Cash dividends have been in an uptrend since they were first paid in 1957. Further, the percent payout is modest to allow a large percentage of earnings to be plowed back into corporate expansion.

The level of the debt structure in the corporation appears to be reasonable. Measured against stockholders' equity, the percentage of long-term debt is low. Note, too, that we do not necessarily need a 10-year record of debt levels. The most recent years are particularly relevant. In this case, the favorable comparison of the past 2 years is valid. Institutional holdings are small.

Summarizing Beta's Super Stock Scorecard:

```
┌─────────── BETA CORPORATIONSUPER ──────────┐
│          STOCK SCORECARD CRITIQUE           │
```

		Score
☑	Size—Satisfactory	—
☑	Unit Sales Volume - rising each year and well above inflation; up 40.7% over CPI since 1962.	15
☑	Pretax Profit Margins - above 10% and rising; deduct 3 points for 1964	12
☑	Return of Stockholders' Equity - above 15% and rising.	30
☑	Relative Earnings Per Share Growth - favorable (+111% vs DJIA +47%)	20
☑	Dividends - risings slightly with low percentage payout.	5
☑	Debt Structure - low, 17% of stockholders' equity.	10
☑	Institutional Holdings - low.	5
☑	Price Earnings Ratio - mixed. Could be rising relative to the market, but inconclusive.	—
	Total Score	97

This looks like a super stock.

In real life, Beta Corporation is Walt Disney Productions, a stock that enjoyed superior performance twice in two decades. The first time was in the early 1950s when the stock moved from a low of 8⅝ in 1954 to a high of 48¾ in 1957. That year the stock moved from over-the-counter trading to a listing on the New York Stock Exchange, and the stock continued its advance. In 1954, the Company was still small. Total revenues were only $11.6 million with net profits of $733,852. Total shares outstanding were 652,840.

During 1957, stockbroker reports were estimating sales above $35 million for the year and a net profit increase of more than 30 percent. Actually, they were right on sales and wrong on profits—net profits were up 39 percent. The new theme park opening in 1955 in California was becoming more important.

Disney would have qualified for super stock status in 1957, but investors would have been buying into an unsustainable momentum. The subsequent years of 1958 and 1959 witnessed a slowdown in sales and earnings growth and, in 1960, the company showed a loss as well as a decline in sales.

What happened is instructive for future stock selection. Haloid Xerox spoiled many investors; its fast growth continued in full vigor, unabated for more than a decade. However, growth trends do not continue indefinitely. Developing a trend line from past statistics and projecting that trend endlessly into the future is an exercise in arithmetic futility. It just doesn't happen that way. There are rarely constant, uninterrupted long-term earnings trends; only episodic bursts of growth, a pause, and then another spurt of growth.

In 1957, Disney was nearing the end of one period of growth. Sales and earnings would continue in an uptrend for 2 more years, but at a much slower rate. The year 1960 was a year of transition from one growth period to another, which proved to be even greater. The 1960 Disney Annual Report indicates that the loss that year was caused by a write-down of inventories and a decline in film revenue and television income. The decline in television income was due to the fact that the "Zorro" and "Mickey Mouse" shows were not televised in 1960. Finally, publications, music, records and other merchandising revenue also declined. The two pieces of good news: Disneyland Park revenues increased and the company bought out the 34.5 percent stock interest in Disneyland held by ABC-Paramount for $7,500,000 in cash and notes. This buyout made Disneyland, Inc. a wholly owned subsidiary.

Ahead, in the late 1960s and early 1970s, would be *Mary Poppins*, continued increases in profitability at Disneyland, and of course, the big profit potential that was in the early planning stages in 1965: Disney World in Florida.

The 1966-67 period proved temporarily uneventful for Disney's earnings, although the stock price continued to move ahead, largely in anticipation of Disney World. Earnings growth resumed in 1968 and, by 1973, a $1,000 investment made in 1966 would have been worth more than $17,000.

Walt Disney puts to rest the claim by some growth stock proponents that you should invest only in technology. One difficulty in technology investing is determining which of today's leaders will also be the technical leaders of tomorrow. Skilled analysts have been known to make wrong judgments on the future. And even if they're right on the technology, they might be wrong on management's ability to carry the technology forward to a profitable conclusion.

Witness the famous example of Sperry Rand versus IBM in the early days of computer development. In the 1950s, experts would have argued that Sperry's Univac Computer was far ahead of anything IBM had or could develop in the near future. But IBM had superb marketing management—enough to give them a winning position early in the game. In the case of Haloid Xerox, we let the statistical record lead us to a conclusion. It was more efficient in time and money, and more effective than analyzing the qualitative aspects of the products.

In the case of Walt Disney, the company and its record had to be analyzed more closely despite the fact that the products, films, books, and theme parks can all be understood by the average investor. Whether we like Snow White or Disneyland has little meaning in terms of Disney's investment qualities. Stripped of emotion, of warm affection for their likable products, Disney emerges as a super stock candidate strictly based on our scorecard characteristics.

CASE 3: GAMMA CORPORATION

Our third super stock exercise concerns a company in a relatively prosaic sector of the packaging business. The time is early 1975. When reviewing the fourth quarter and year-end results for 1974, you are struck by the annual report of our third case study: Gamma Corporation. In a recession year with poor earnings results the norm, Gamma has reported 1974 earnings of $2.20 per share. This is up more than 21 percent over the 1973 results of $1.81 per share. Gamma's record is one of the few significant sales and earnings increases you have seen in several weeks of reviewing numerous 1974 operating results. However, total sales in 1974 exceeded our $500 million size limit. But Gamma is only the fourth largest manufacturer in its field with less than 10 percent of its industry revenues. The record suggests that this company is definitely worth investigating for super stock possibilities.

The analysis of the financial record reaffirms our suspicions. This is the earnings per share record for the past 10 years:

Year	Earnings per Share
1974	$2.20
1973	1.81
1972	1.58
1971	1.41
1970	1.26
1969	1.11
1968	1.01
1967	.91
1966	.80
1965	.71

Earnings increased each year for the last 10 years. Even beyond that, an inspection of the record back into the 1950s indicated no evidence of a "down year." Moreover, Gamma weathered the recession of 1967 and 1970 nicely. A remarkable performance. A study of the annual reports and other financial data sources reveal the following information for the analysis:

- Standard & Poor's or other authoritative sources indicated institutional holdings for Gamma as follows: 26 institutions owned a total of 1.4 million shares (8% of the outstanding stock).

- Further research shows that price earnings ratio, while declining, has been gradually improving relative to the market:

	Gamma P/E Ratio		Dow Industrials P/E	
	High	*Low*	*High*	*Low*
1974	9.6x	6.2x	9.0x	5.8x
1973	15.8	10.6	12.2	9.1
1972	17.4	11.7	15.4	13.2
1971	16.6	12.3	17.3	14.5

GAMMA CORPORATION SELECTED FINANCIAL DATA
(Thousands of Dollars)

	1974	1973	1972	1971	1970	1969	1968	1967	1966
Sales/Gross Revenues	$766,158	$571,762	$448,880	$448,446	$414,161	$370,903	$337,118	$301,147	$279,830
Pre-tax Income	72,961	61,013	56,093	53,034	52,628	47,805	42,291	33,366	29,429
Income Tax	33,298	26,725	24,900	24,560	26,770	24,800	21,389	14,529	12,880
Net Income	39,663	34,288	31,193	28,474	25,858	23,005	20,902	18,837	16,749
Dividends (Common)									
Long Term Debt	34,413	37,922	31,234	41,680	37,490	36,271	40,871	56,131	57,890
Stockholders' Equity	262,650	243,916	230,366	211,847	193,508	172,937	150,105	129,567	110,841
Common Shares Outstanding (Thousands)	18,001	18,894	19,727	20,212	20,408	20,659	20,641	20,634	20,607
Per Share ($)									
Net Income	2.20	1.81	1.58	1.41	1.26	1.11	1.00	.91	.80
Dividends	—	—	—	—	—	—	—	—	—

┌─────────── **GAMMA CORPORATION** ───────────┐
│   **SUPER STOCK SCORECARD**

                                              Score

☐ Size .... (Confirm)

☐ Unit Sales Volume......................

☐ Pretax Profit Margins...................

☐ Return on Stockholders' Equity...........

☐ Relative Earnings Per Share Growth........

☐ Dividends..............................

☐ Debt Structure.........................

☐ Institutional Holdings...................

☐ Price Earnings Ratio.............   (Confirm)

                            Total

```
┌─────────────── GAMMA CORPORATION ───────────────┐
│               SUPER STOCK SCORECARD CRITIQUE      │
│                                                   │
│                                            Score  │
│                                          ───────  │
│  ☞  Size - big in terms of sales, but acceptable  │
│     related to the industry.                  —   │
│                                                   │
│  ☞  Unit Sales Volume—rising trend and above      │
│     inflation, except in 1972. Deduct 5 points.  10│
│                                                   │
│  ☞  Pretax Profit Margins—below 10% and not in a  │
│     favorable trend, even considering the         │
│     recession.                                0   │
│                                                   │
│  ☞  Return on Stockholders' Equity—a somewhat     │
│     favorable trend, but watch out! What will     │
│     happen to the sales and earnings growth rates │
│     if management ever decides to pay a dividend? │
│     A 15 % ROE is not enough!                 30  │
│                                                   │
│  ☞  Relative Earnings Per Share Growth—unfavorable│
│     (+56% vs. DJIA +80%).                      0  │
│                                                   │
│  ☞  Dividends—none. Definite negative for a       │
│     company at this stage. It is easier to be     │
│     forgiving with new or younger companies.   0  │
│                                                   │
│  ☞  Debt Structure—low; a positive rating.    10  │
│  ☞  Institutional Holdings—acceptable.         5  │
│  ☞  Price Earnings Ratio—declining, but           │
│     performing better than the market.         —  │
│                                                 ───│
│                                      Total     55 │
│                                                ═══│
└───────────────────────────────────────────────────┘
```

Conclusion: Gamma Corporation is a growth stock, but not a super stock. Size is a negative, but not fatal. Pretax profitability is a question. Normally, the lack of a dividend is not crucial for a new company. But this is not a new company. However, management's stated policy of not paying a dividend is a major drawback. Moreover, a closer look at the figures reveals only a 12 percent average compounded growth rate in pretax income over the past 8 years—despite plowing every penny back into the company! Finally, as explained in Chapter 3, any company with a 100 percent plowback can grow internally no faster than its return on equity will allow, in this case, 14 to 15 percent per year. This is *without* any dividend. What will happen if they decide, as they should, to pay one?

Gamma Corporation was not deemed to be a super stock and its stock price performance proved to be satisfactory, but unspectacular, in the years following this study. Actually, the company is Crown Cork and Seal, a major factor in the container industry where it has positioned itself in fast-growing markets. Crown Cork is a good example of excellent financial growth, but not quite making it in the super stock category.

CASE 4: DELTA CORPORATION

The fourth case study represents the genesis of a basically one-product company. The time: March, 1968. By reading the financial section of the morning paper you notice the 1967 results of our example. Delta Corporation. Sales are reported at $36.9 million, up 16 percent over 1966, and net income increased 3.4 percent to $3,714,000. Not too bad for a recession period.

Though not spectacular, what catches your eye is the comment about the last half of 1967: sales up 35 percent and earnings up 20 percent from the year-earlier period. It is not a bad idea to read more than the first paragraph of a news release. Further, you read that Delta's 1967 sales were near by *10 times* greater than the company's sales 10 years ago, and that net earnings were more than *30 times* larger than earnings in 1957. Delta seems to be just the right size with superior operating results. Could Delta be a super stock?

In addition to the financial data, additional information on price earnings ratios and institutional holdings could be found from traditional sources:

	Delta P/E Ratio		Dow Industrials P/E	
	High	*Low*	*High*	*Low*
1967	22.4x	9.4x	17.5x	14.6x
1966	15.4	7.6	17.3	12.9
1965	16.4	10.1	18.1	15.7
1964	15.3	11.6	19.2	16.5

DELTA CORPORATION SELECTED FINANCIAL DATA
(Thousands of Dollars)

	1967	1966	1965	1964	1963	1962	1961	1960	1959	1958
Net Sales	$36,928	$31,010	$24,056	$18,184	$14,370	$10,804	$6,824	$6,417	$5,550	$3,975
Pre-tax Income	7,079	6,790	6,021	5,109	3,817	2,836	1,575	968	713	213
Income Tax	3,365	3,203	2,846	2,582	2,002	1,442	806	492	360	94
Net Income	3,714	3,587	3,175	2,527	1,815	1,394	769	476	353	119
Dividends (Common)	621	569	500	402	327	148	110	73	55	44
Long Term Debt	3,300	—	—	—	—	—	—	53	143	58
Stockholders' Equity	17,773	14,677	11,653	8,965	6,552	5,042	3,768	3,109	2,706	2,400
Common Shares Outstanding (Thousands)	2,524	2,517	2,510	2,498	2,250	2,230	2,202	2,202	2,202	2,202
Per Share ($)										
Net Income	1.47	1.43	1.27	1.01	.81	.62	.34	.21	.16	.05
Dividends	.25	.23	.20	.16	.15	.07	.05	.03	.03	.02

Standard & Poor's Monthly Stock Handbook showed that 8 institutions owned 266,000 shares, or 10.5 percent.

DELTA CORPORATION
SUPER STOCK SCORECARD

	Score
☐ Size	(Confirm)
☐ Unit Sales Volume......................	
☐ Pretax Profit Margins...................	
☐ Return on Stockholders' Equity............	
☐ Relative Earnings Per Share Growth........	
☐ Dividends..............................	
☐ Debt Structure.........................	
☐ Institutional Holdings....................	
☐ Price Earnings Ratio....................	(Confirm)
Total	_____

——————— DELTA CORPORATION ———————
SUPER STOCK SCORECARD CRITIQUE

		Score
☑	Size—approaching $50 million—a good size.	—
☑	Unit Sales Volume—rising significantly faster than inflation. Double check for acquisitions.	15
☑	Pretax Profit Margins—well above 10% and rising longer term. A poor trend in 1965-1967 period (deduct 9 points), but now showing definite signs of rising.	6
☑	Return on Stockholders' Equity—still well above 15 % and rising. Compared to prior recession (1960, 1958) years, 1967 showed substantial progress and very recent figures suggest improvement ahead.	30
☑	Relative Earnings Per Share Growth— favorable (+45% vs. DJIA + 16%).	20
☑	Dividends—small payout, trend is up.	5
☑	Debt Structure—low position	10
☑	Institutional Holdings—low and acceptable, but not as low as we'd like.	2
☑	Price Earnings Ratios—rising.	—
	Total	88

Conclusion: A possible super stock. Or, at the very lest, this stock deserves further analysis. Good growth rates in both sales and earnings seem likely to continue. Delta Corporation appears to be performing well in a poor environment. Furthermore, the company's operations are, even now, quite profitable and could be getting better.

Our hypothetical Delta Corporation is in actuality Masco Corporation, a major producer of single-handled faucets, the "Delta" faucets with a patented mechanism. In 1967, more than 20 million faucets of all kinds were sold, of which 25 percent were single-handled faucets and Masco was the leading producer of this product.

The obvious question to be asked at this point is: Will the market for faucets of this type be saturated any time soon? And what is the company's ability to develop or acquire new products? You notice by reading the annual report that Masco acquired another business in 1967. In the report, management states that this acquisition is one significant reason for the decline in pretax margins and ROE in the most recent year. Now, it appears, Masco's profitability could be even better than the figures suggested at first glance.

How well did this investment fare? Five years later, in 1972, Masco reported earnings of $14.4 million on sales of $134 million. Earlier that year, the stock reached a price of $65½, up 400 percent from the adjusted March, 1968 price of $13. Today, Masco has sales approaching $1 billion and in recent years, the stock has been above $40 per share after another 2 for 1 stock split in 1975.

CASE 5: EPSILON CORPORATION

The time is May, 1970 and for one entire evening you've been looking through a book of stock charts for new ideas. Almost every stock is down. As an initial filter, you decide to consider only those stocks that: (1) Have declined by about 50 percent or more from prices of 3 to 6 months earlier; (2) Are under $500 million in sales; (3) Are showing increases in earnings in both the past year and in the most recent quarter; (4) Have little or no long-term debt; and (5) Have pretax profit margins of at lest 15 percent.

In the search, it hasn't been difficult to find stocks that have declined 50 percent. However, finding companies that are showing any earnings increases, let alone 15 percent margins, is becoming quite a bit more of a challenge! Most of the drug companies seem to show earnings gains, but then few are down 50 percent in price. Many of the technology companies are down 50 percent, but so are their earnings. The desire for little or no debt is due to concern over the recent trend of sharply higher interest rates. However, one that passed the filter is a company we'll call Epsilon Corporation. Total 1969 revenues are reported at $434,503,000 up a modest 4 percent from the $418,620,000 reported in 1968. Net income of $4.00 per share was up 13 percent over the 1968 net of $3.55 per share, adjusted for the 3 for 2 stock split in May, 1969. The report also says that 1969 set a new record for Epsilon, both in revenues and earnings. In addition, the first quarter in 1970 also showed gains.

A quick check of the company's record indicates that the company is positioned in an attractive segment of a major natural resource industry. Revenues increased more than 32 percent from $318.1 million in 1965 to $420.6 million in 1969. And earnings per share went up even more rapidly, from $2.34 per share in 1965 to $4.00 in 1969, a 71 percent increase.

But what about size? Last year's sales were more than $420 million. That would seem to indicate Epsilon could already be too large to show significant increases in sales and earnings in future years. We would prefer a smaller company, but remember "large" and "small" are not absolutes; they are relative standards. Size depends on the company in its industry context. A $400 million sales company in a business serving a multi-billion-dollar market would not be considered big. And a review of Epsilon Corporation indicates that it is basically a service company supplying essential needs to huge companies positioned in the resource extraction business.

Beyond size, the question is: Does this company match our requirements for a super stock? If we assume that only 5 years of key reference data are available, is it possible to make an evaluation? The operating and stock data are presented here in summary form.

EPSILON CORPORATION SELECTED FINANCIAL DATA
(Millions of Dollars)

	1969	1968	1967	1966	1965
Net Sales/Revenue	$420.6	$409.1	$369.2	$343.1	$318.1
Pre-tax Income	74.8	68.3	52.0	49.3	47.7
Income Tax	28.5	27.3	20.5	21.1	20.6
Net Income	46.3	41.0	31.5	28.1	27.1
Dividends (Common)	16.0	11.6	9.2	8.9	7.7
Long Term Debt	—	—	8.9	11.8	12.4
Stockholders' Equity	344.3	321.3	293.6	266.8	252.6
Common Shares Outstanding	11,565	11,600	11,543	11,394	11,540
Per Share ($)					
Net Income	4.00	3.55	2.75	2.45	2.34
Dividends	1.28	0.95	0.80	0.78	0.67

In addition, here is information not contained in the five-year summary:

1). The rate of return on stockholders' equity for all corporations in the U.S. was 11.9 percent in 1969. In Epsilon's particular industry it was 14.2 percent.
2). A check of institutional holdings indicates that in 1969 fifteen institutions held 488,000 shares or 4.2 percent of the stock.
3). The company's price earnings ratio record was as follows:

| | Epsilon P/E Ratio | | Dow Industrials P/E | |
	High	Low	High	Low
1969	27.5x	19.1x	17.0x	13.5x
1968	25.8	13.0	17.0	14.3
1967	18.2	9.8	17.5	14.6
1966	16.4	10.7	17.3	12.9
1965	15.6	12.5	18.1	15.7

Now you are ready to analyze the operating record of Epsilon and see how it rates on the Super Stock Score Card.

EPSILON CORPORATION
SUPER STOCK SCORECARD

Score

☐ Size .... (Confirm)

☐ Unit Sales Volume.......................

☐ Pretax Profit Margins....................

☐ Return on Stockholders' Equity............

☐ Relative Earnings Per Share Growth........

☐ Dividends...............................

☐ Debt Structure...........................

☐ Institutional Holdings....................

☐ Price Earnings Ratio..................... (Confirm)

Total _____

─────EPSILON CORPORATION─────
SUPER STOCK SCORECARD CRITIQUE

Score

☑ Size—big in terms of sales figures, but not too large relative to its industry. —

☑ Sales Volume—rising above CPI each year, except for 1969. Overall, sales rose 8.8% above the inflation rate (1966-69). 10

☑ Pretax Profit Margins—above 10%; rising, without any major decline. Deduct 3 points for 1967. 12

☑ Return on Stockholders' Equity—rising and 15% does not appear impossible. 25

☑ Relative Earnings Per Share Growth— favorable (+63 % vs. DJIA −1%). 20

☑ Dividends—rising dividends with a low payout ratio. 5

☑ Debt Structure—not significant in 1970. 10

☑ Institutional Holdings—favorable 5

☑ Price Earnings Ratio—a rising trend, improving versus the market. —

Total 87

Conclusion: Epsilon Corporation is a possible super stock. The company is engaged in a promising business and any meaningful sales growth following this difficult economic period could lead to substantial earnings improvement and a sharply higher stock price.

In this example, Epsilon Corporation is, in actual corporate life, Schlumberger, Ltd., a technically-oriented company supplying wireline services to the petroleum industry including geological services, contract drilling, and other oil well services. The company also manufactures electronic equipment and instrument control systems.

Had Schlumberger been identified in early 1970 through 1975, the company would have fulfilled our wildest expectations. Total operating revenues from sales and services in 1975 were $1.6 billion, compared to $421 million in 1969, while net income increased to $219.3 million, compared to $46.3 million in 1969. More to the point, adjusted for two splits during the period, earnings per share increased from 89 cents to $3.92 and the stock price rose from under $12 to nearly $100. This performance is impressive considering the period 1970 through 1975 encompassed one really bad stock market experience in 1973 to 74.

However, there was no particular reason to sell Schlumberger at the end of 1975. All of the super stock indicators were still intact—rising sales, increasing margins, return on equity, and so on. The three growing negatives were its size, an increasing debt, and the widening institutional participation. Still, by late 1980, the stock reached as high as $130 (after three more splits), compared with the adjusted prices of $30 in 1975 and a low in 1970 of under $4.

CASE 6: ZETA COMPANY

It is late spring in 1982 and you are hard at work with your weekly review of the 1981 year-end earnings reports in the Wall Street Journal. You are searching, as usual, for unusual earnings increases. Once again, you are applying your financial criteria for further detailed investigation. You have decided to consider only those stocks that have:

- sales under $500 million

- significant earnings increases in 1981 and in the most recent quarter

- minimum of long term debt

- unit sales volume rising faster than inflation

- rising pretax profit margins.

Your eye falls on an unusual set of corporate figures for a retailing company. Sales for the year ending January 31, 1982 were

$2,445,000,000, up from $1,643,000,000 in 1981. That's a 1-year sales growth of more than $800 million—a 49 percent increase! Remarkable for a billion dollar plus company. In addition, Zeta's sales volume is only a fraction of the huge megabillions common in the retailing business.

You read further and learn that Zeta Company is a discount retailer; that sales in 1978 were a mere $678 million. In 3 years sales have increased a dramatic 260 percent. Therefore, you can conclude that despite its large size, Zeta is growing faster than most growth companies and is worth investigating. As in the case of the previous Epsilon Corporation (Schlumberger, Ltd.), "large" and "small" are not absolutes.

A further review of Zeta's record (conducted by reading the annual report that we had requested by mail) reflects growing profitability, as shown below:

Year Ending Jan. 31	Sales Million $	Net Income Million $
1982	2,445	83
1981	1,643	56
1980	1,248	41
1979	900	29
1978	678	22

Detailed reading of the annual report and recent quarterly statements indicates that Zeta operates and is establishing new discount stores in small towns primarily in southern, southwestern, and midwestern states. Each store features more than a dozen departments including family apparel, automotive supplies, housewares, sporting goods, hardware, and health and beauty aids. Additionally, the company features both nationally advertised brands as well as private-label items. Apparently Zeta has found a "niche" in the discount retailing business that will allow it to grow without competing head-to-head with the giant chains such as K Mart, Woolworth (Woolco), and Sears.

Further, you reflect on the number of small towns in the growing southern and southwestern states and you begin to realize that, despite the more than $2.4 billion in sales in fiscal 1982, there is still plenty of room for the company to double and redouble its size.

You note one final point: last year's sales profit performance was accomplished in a period of deepening recession. By spring of 1982 it was apparent that the economy as measured by the Gross National Product was declining with unemployment rising (it was soon to reach 10 percent), and interest rates continuing to be high. All of this was reflected in a still-falling stock market.

Certainly there is opportunity here, but the essential question is: Does the company match our requirements for a super stock? We again turn to the annual report and review the data presented in the 4-year summary. Is it possible to make an initial judgment based solely on these figures? The operating and per-share data excerpted from Zeta's 1982 financial report is as shown.

ZETA CORPORATION
SELECTED FINANCIAL DATA
(Millions of Dollars)

	1978	1979	1980	1981	1982
Net Sales/Revenues	$678	$900	$1,248	$1,643	$3,376
Pretax Income	42	57	74	99	149
Pretax Profit Margin	.062	.063	.060	.060	.044
Net Income	22	29	41	56	83
Long-Term Debt	32	98	122	165	259
Stockholders Equity	99	127	165	248	323

In addition, we find that the rate of return on stockholders' equity for Zeta Company was as follows:

Year	Return on Equity
1982	28.9%
1981	26.2%
1980	28.1%
1979	25.9%
1978	25.6%

That's an extraordinary performance in the retailing business far and above the average operation and well above the average for most American Corporations.

Finally, we review the price earnings ratio record:

	ZETA P/E RATIO		DOW INDUSTRIALS P/E	
	High	*Low*	*High*	*Low*
1982 (1st half)	18	11	11.3*	11.3*
1981	18	8	9.0	7.4
1980	14	8	8.2	6.2
1979	15	9	7.2	6.4

*Actual P/E - per share earnings for 12 months ended June 30, 1982 divided by price on June 30, 1982.

You also note that in this bear market of 1982, the P/E ratio is currently well below its highest level. At this point you are ready to analyze the operating record of Zeta Company and judge how it will reflect on the Super Stock Scorecard.

ZETA COMPANY
SUPER STOCK SCORECARD

Score

☐ Size

☐ Unit Sales Volume   (Confirm)

☐ PreTax Profit Margins

☐ Dividends

☐ Debt Structure

☐ Institutional Holdings

☐ Price Earnings Ratio   (Confirm)

Total _____

ZETA COMPANY
SUPER STOCK SCORECARD CRITIQUE

	Score
☑ *Size*—big in terms of sales but not relative to the industry. Not a negative.	0
☑ *Sales Volume*—rising well above the CPI each year.	15
☑ *Pretax Profit Margins*—generally stabilized since 1978 at .06% with exception of the recession year of 1982.	15
☑ *Return on Stockholders Equity*—significantly above our 15% target. Maximum points should be rewarded.	30
☑ *Relative Earnings Per Share Growth*—favorable.	20
☑ *Dividends*—have been paid since 1973 and are rising.	
☑ *Debt Structure*—company's long term debt is well above 50% of stockholders equity. Not unusual for a fast growing retail operation. Nevertheless, no points are awarded.	0
☑ *Institutional Holdings*—more than 15 percent.	0
☑ *Price Earnings Ratio*—a rising trend, improving relative to the market.	0
Total	85

Conclusion: Zeta Company, with a score of 85 points, is a potential super stock. It is positioned in an essential and growing service business with an interesting specialty ''niche''—discount stores in small towns of growing states. Its record to 1982 reflects growing acceptance of the Zeta's concept.

In this example, Zeta Company is the almost legendary retail company: Wal-Mart Stores. Its unique expansion approach, coupled with an aggressive pricing policy, allowed the company to gain market share right through the 1980s. In fact, by the end of fiscal 1988, sales had reached nearly $12 billion ($11,909,000,000), with a net income of nearly half a billion dollars ($450,000,000), reflecting the more than 1,114 Wal-Mart stores it operates.

Even at that point, Wal-Mart is seeking out new retailing concepts. Sam's Wholesale Club, for example, began in April, 1983 as a "membership only," cash and carry wholesale warehouse operating in metropolitan areas. By early 1988, there were 84 of these stores (or more properly, retail concepts) in operation. And the newest concept—the huge hypermarket—was under development.

If you had identified Wal-Mart in the spring of 1982 and finally, after many weeks of analysis, decided to buy it in early August of that year, you would have seen sales increased from the $2.5 billion in 1982 to $3.4 billion in 1983, and ultimately to $11.9 billion in 1987. Further, earnings per share grew from 16 cents, recorded in 1982, to $1.11 in 1988. The modest annual dividend increased more than six-fold and that all-important price of the stock went from an adjusted low of 2⅞ to a price of 32 in mid-July of 1988*. All of this despite the searing bear market in the Fall of 1987!

Further, there would have been no reason to sell Wal-Mart in the period between the summer of 1982 up to the summer of 1988 since sales, profit margins, and earnings per share continued to increase. (This occurred in spite of the comments of some retail analysts who have repeatedly warned that sooner or later the growth would stop.) It hasn't yet as the record shows!

---

*Stock splits of 100% in July, 1982, Oct., 1985 and July, 1987.

WAL-MART STORES
Stock Price
(1982-1988)

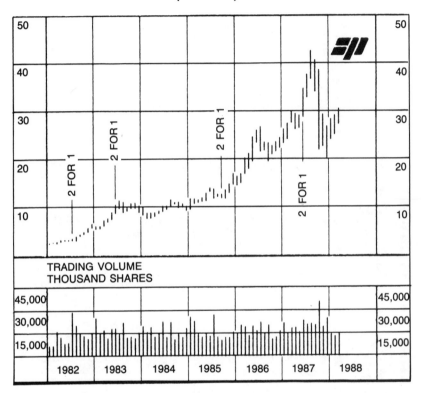

BRISTOL-MYERS COMPANY
Portrait of a Super Stock 1957 to 1967

Year	Sales ($mm)	Pretax Margin %	Net Income ($000)	Return On Avg. Equity %	-Per Earn.	Share Div.	Payout Ratio %	LT Debt % of Equity	Average Stock Price $	Average P/E Ratio
1952	$ 56.6	8.9%	$ 2,589	7.6%	$0.13	$0.14	108%	39%	2 1/2	20.0x
1953	55.5	9.1%	2,541	6.9%	0.12	0.08	69%	38%	1 7/8	15.4
1954	62.4	11.6%	3,604	9.5%	0.18	0.08	46%	35%	2 1/4	12.8
1955	75.7	12.1%	4,866	12.4%	0.25	0.13	51%	33%	2 5/8	10.5
1956	89.4	12.2%	5,586	14.0%	0.30	0.15	49%	29%	3 1/8	10.3
1957	106.8	13.3%	6,404	15.3%	0.34	0.17	49%	25%	4 1/2	12.5
1958	113.9	12.0%	7,235	15.3%	0.37	0.18	49%	21%	5 1/2	14.9
1959	131.5	14.1%	8,889	15.6%	0.43	0.22	50%	16%	8 7/8	20.6
1960	146.7	15.7%	10,768	16.3%	0.52	0.26	51%	13%	13 1/8	25.2
1961	164.4	16.9%	12,957	17.9%	0.62	0.30	49%	10%	21	33.9
1962	198.8	17.3%	16,094	20.0%	0.77	0.38	49%	8%	20 1/8	26.1
1963	232.4	17.9%	19,132	21.2%	0.91	0.45	49%	5%	26 3/8	29.0
1964	265.0	18.1%	23,095	22.7%	1.09	0.53	49%	4%	32 3/8	29.7
1965	391.4	16.6%	33,357	26.6%	1.32	0.65	49%	—	41 3/4	31.6
1966	468.5	17.1%	39,402	26.2%	1.57	0.75	48%	—	50 1/8	31.5
1967	730.1	13.7%	52,019	25.0%	1.86	0.95	51%	30%	67 7/8	36.5
1968	827.0	13.9%	57,120	20.7%	1.96	1.10	56%	27%	71 3/8	36.4
1969	928.2	14.2%	67,606	21.5%	2.23	1.20	54%	23%	64 1/2	28.9
1970	981.2	14.5%	74,112	20.8%	2.41	1.20	50%	43%	61 3/8	25.5
1971	1,066.4	13.2%	75,767	18.9%	2.44	1.20	49%	38%	63 1/8	25.9
1972	1,201.2	12.6%	83,935	18.5%	2.60	1.20	46%	27%	64 5/8	24.8
Growth Rate*	21.2%		23.3%		18.8%	18.8%			31.2%	

Note: Stock Splits...3 for 1 in 1959; 2 for 1 in 1963; 2 for 1 in 1966   *Average 1957-67.

William McLaren Bristol   *John Ripley Myers*

CASE 7: BRISTOL-MYERS COMPANY

Without using a fictitious name, let's look at Bristol-Myers Company as our final case study. The business was founded in 1887 by William M. Bristol and John R. Myers with an initial investment of $5,000. After 70 years, the company reached $100 million in sales and, 14 years after that, $1 billion. But within that 14-year span, actually from 1957 to 1967, Bristol-Myers was indeed a super stock. Over this 11-year period, the stock price advanced an average of 31 percent per year—not including the added benefit of dividends. That Magic Combination was in full force! Now, let's go back in time.

It's early 1957. BMC shares are about $45 on the New York Stock Exchange. The earnings report for 1956, which has just been released, indicates profits of $3.54 per share, up 19 percent from the $2.97 per share of 1955. At the current price, the stock is valued at about 11 times estimated 1957 earnings, while the dividend yield is a little better than 4 percent. The company has a modest amount of debt, the pretax margin is a respectable 12 percent, and the return on stockholders' equity appears to be approaching 15 percent. Not bad!

A closer look at the company's financial statements reveals that cash and marketable securities, nearly $15 million, comfortably exceed total current liabilities of $9 million, while the current ratio (total current assets divided by total current liabilities) is better than 3 to 1—another healthy sign. Also interesting is that Bristol-Myers' advertising, selling and administrative expenses represent the largest cost item on the income statement. These are, for the most part, variable costs that can be managed. Moreover, the cost of sales figure, only about one-third of sales, has been rising less rapidly than sales. In short, the company's profitability appears good and could be getting better if the products sell.

Bristol-Myers' sales in 1956 were classified into three or four major categories, the most important being Toiletries & Cosmetics (39%), Proprietary Medicines (32%), and Prescription Medicines (18%). Research expenditures, about $3.2 million that year, seemed to be divided between the Products Division, which is now enjoying success with its new *Ban* roll-on deodorant, and the Bristol Laboratories Division, which has just recently introduced *Tetrex*, an improved tetracycline antibiotic. Clearly, more new products seem likely. In addition, it appears that management is interested in expanding the product line further through acquisitions.

Would it have been possible for an investor in 1957 to know that Bristol-Myers could be another super stock? What do you think?

Now, with nearly four decades of 20/20 hindsight, can we in the 1980s and 1990s expect to profit from the lessons and the case studies cited here? Yes, with a little work! And Finding The Next Super Stock will make that effort worthwhile!

He who fights and runs away,
lives to fight another day.
ANONYMOUS

7

Bear Market Investing

MOST OF US HAVE READ AND REREAD THE STORY OF THE CRASH OF 1929: how the entire financial world staggered in disbelief over the fact that in 5 trading days, the Dow Jones Industrial Average had lost more than 47 percent of its value. By the time the decline ended in late 1932, the Dow had fallen 89 percent from its high of 1929. And all investors have been fascinated that not until 1954, 25 years later, was the Dow Jones Industrial Average able to match the levels of early October 1929!

BEAR MARKETS OF THE PAST

From 1929 to 1988, there have been 13 bear markets, ranging from the sudden and swift decline of 1937 to a 37 percent decline in the 6 weeks of the 1987 crash. Among these bear markets was a swift and sudden one in 1937, others in 1939–1942, 1946, 1957, 1960, 1962, 1966, 1973–1974, 1977–1978, 1981–1982, and the crash of 1987–1988.

The longest of these bear markets was the one that followed the crash of 1929, which lasted 34 months. The shortest was the 6-month bear market that started in 1961. The average bear market in this

THE 30 STOCKS IN THE
DOW JONES INDUSTRIAL AVERAGE*

Name	Business
1. Allied-Signal	Chemicals & Electronics
2. Alcoa	Aluminum
3. American Express	Financial Services
4. American Telephone & Telegraph	Telecommunications
5. Bethlehem Steel	Integrated Steel Producer
6. Boeing	Aircraft
7. Chevron	Oil
8. Coca Cola	Beverages
9. DuPont	Chemicals & Oil
10. Eastman Kodak	Chemicals
11. Exxon	Oil
12. General Electric	Electric Equipment Manufacturer Financing Services
13. General Motors	Automotive
14. Goodyear	Rubber
15. IBM	Computers
16. International Paper	Paper Products
17. McDonalds	Fast Food
18. Merck	Pharmaceuticals
19. Minnesota Mining & Manufacturing	Diversified Manufacturer of Industrial and Consumer Products
20. Navistar	Conglomerate
21. Phillip Morris	Cigarette Manufacturer and Diversified Consumer Products
22. Primerica	Financial Services
23. Proctor & Gamble	Consumer Goods
24. Sears Roebuck	Retailing & Financial Services
25. Texaco	Oil
26. USX	Steel & Oil
27. Union Carbide	Chemicals
28. United Technologies	Defense/Electronics
29. Westinghouse	Electric Equipment & Electronics
30. Woolworth	Retailing

*As of 1988

country has been just over 19 months—roughly half the life of an average bull market.

Nevertheless, reviewing the history of bear markets puts into question the attractiveness of stock market investing. Why go through all that pain and agony? Should you as an investor be in the stock market at all? The answer starts with another question: Can you afford *not* to be? Viewed long term, the stock market has provided greater returns than any other major asset type. For example, in the 60-year period between 1926 and 1986, common stocks had a total annual return of 12.1 percent, compared with returns of 5.3 percent for corporate bonds, 4.7 percent for government bonds, and 3.5 percent for Treasury bills. During that same period, consumer prices rose at an average rate of 3.1 percent per year. Measured over this 60-year period, common stocks outperformed bonds nearly 2½ to 1 and beat inflation by more than 4 to 1.

Of course, stocks are also riskier than other assets. That's the price you pay for their increased returns. The 13 bear markets of this century, particularly the market declines of 1962, 1973, 1981, and the fall of 1987, simply emphasize the risks involved in stock market

Stock Market Returns Over Varying Time Periods
(S&P 500 Stock Index 1926-1986)

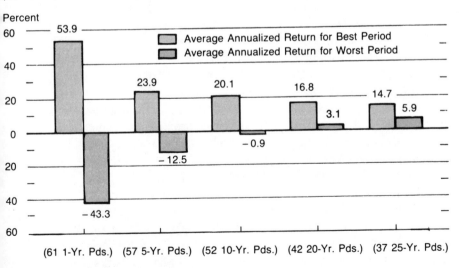

Source: Computer Directions Advisors.

investing. The bull markets that followed each downturn also multiplied the profits. For these reasons, it is instructive to examine the structure of the last big bear market (fall of 1987) in some detail and depth.

THE GREAT OCTOBER CRASH OF 1987

On Monday, October 19, 1987, the U.S. stock market simply collapsed. In 1 day, the Dow Jones Industrial Average plunged 22.6 percent (the worst 1-day loss ever) on record volume. Some 47 million investors in the stock market lost ⅕th of their stock value during just a few trading hours, and the financial damage was startling. Sam Walton, the largest stockholder of Wal-mart, a department store chain, lost $1 billion on that day. More philosophical than most, he said, "It was paper when we started, and it's paper afterward." Others were less stoic. As one Wall Street trader noted, "It's as if an entire bear market, which usually lasts at least 6 months, was compressed into 1 trading day!"

How could such a downturn happen so suddenly? By August 1987, the Dow had reached a new all-time high. Yet in late October, the Dow plummeted to an all-time, 1-day low! From the highs of August to the lows of October, (a span of less than 8 weeks), the market averages lost more than 36 percent of their value. To understand why this happened, it is necessary to put "Black Monday" into perspective, examining its causes and its lessons for individual investors.

With the wreckage of the stock market's crash still apparent, it is hard to recall that the Dow's rocket upward was almost as remarkable as its 1-day plunge. For the year 1987, the Dow Jones Industrial Average gained 42.88 points, or 2.26 percent, and closed at 1,938.83. But that modest, incremental upswing tells nothing of the stormy year of 1987, which was one of exceptional contrasts. The market fed and then shattered illusions, beginning with great promise, then stumbling in the late spring, churning its way through a spectacular summer rally and then collapsing in October's panic.

But back to the beginning: January, 1987. The market was still enjoying its greatest rally ever, a surge that could be traced back to mid-August of 1982, when the Federal Reserve began cutting interest rates to help pull the economy out of a recession. In August of that recession year, the Dow stood at 776.92, some 225 points *below* its peak 10 years before! By February 1983, the Dow had hit its first four-digit mark in more than 10 years, breaking the 1,000 mark to a high of 1,100. From then on, it was shattering one record after another, closing out 1986 at 1,895.95. On January 8, 1987 the Dow broke 2,000.

Reaching the 2,000-mark had taken only 4 years, while the 1,000-mark was elusive for more than 10 years, during the 1970s and early 1980s. Clearly, the Dow was snowballing. On January 19, 1987, the 2,100 mark was reached. In fact, the Dow rose on 13 consecutive days during January—a record! On April 6, it hit 2,400 and analysts and investors were enthralled by the possibilities for the future. Elation continued and the Dow reached 2,722.42 on August 25, some 12 days after this bull market turned 5 years old.

But as some experts were forecasting that the market would continue to soar to new heights in 1987, others were growing nervous, in part because the blue-chip Dow was doing even better than the overall market. The longevity of the bull market bothered many analysts, and its volatility and volume, which many attributed to computer-assisted program trading, were also viewed with alarm by some.

In the end, the "gloomsters" were right and the "bulls" were wrong. There was a change in command at the Federal Reserve, and Alan Greenspan replaced Paul A. Volcker as Federal Reserve chairman in August 1987. Mr. Greenspan tightened monetary policy and one result was an upward pressure on interest rates. By mid-October, investors began to view the rising rates with alarm. They believed that high rates and a still-weak dollar were both bad news for stocks. On that fateful Monday, October 19th, sell orders were everywhere on Wall Street, and panic rocked the financial markets.

What precipitated the great crash of the fall of 1987 will be debated by financial historians for decades to come. While most of the blame was placed on a deadly trio of problems—a relentlessly high Federal budget deficit, a rising trade deficit, and a declining dollar—this doesn't answer the question of why the German (Frankfurt) stock market fell more than the American markets. West Germany had none of the problems of a budget deficit, trade deficit, or a declining currency that the U.S. did.

One explanation is provided by one of the many studies that examined the crash, the GAO (General Accounting Office) study. As the independent investigative arm of Congress, the GAO is an impartial auditor of the federal bureaucracy, and because it is considered independent of political influence, its recommendations carry considerable weight.

After the market plunged in October, the GAO was asked by Congress to conduct an analysis of the crash. According to its report released in early 1988, computerized trading aggravated the selling panic on October 19th and affected the market far more extensively than was previously believed.

According to the GAO, on October 19th, temporary breakdowns affected 9 of the 12 major computer systems—6 of those 9 were directly responsible for executing stock trades—and hundreds of trades could not be completed. This lag appears to have accelerated the plunge in stock prices by adding more uncertainty and confusion to the market on the day the Dow Jones Industrial Average fell 508 points. Proof of this can be found in the actions of some of the large sellers on that fateful Black Monday. For example, the General Motors pension fund (the largest corporate pension fund in the U.S. with about $30 billion in assets) sold at least $1.1 billion in stocks during that 1 day. Not only was the amount enormous in size, but the manner in which this amount of stock was sold was devastating to the market: 13 selling "spasms" of nearly $100 million each hit the market between 10:30 A.M. and 2:00 P.M. on that day.

Another big seller was the Fidelity Group of mutual funds. Because of shareholders' redemptions on the preceding Friday (October 16) and telephone switching that Monday morning, Fidelity Investments was forced to sell nearly $800 million in stock. The GAO study, as well as others, added fresh insight into how precariously close to an entire shutdown the stock market was on October 19.

The GAO also criticized federal regulators, including the Securities and Exchange Commission and the Commodities Futures Trading Commission, for not having developed a contingency plan for handling a stock market crisis. The GAO urged Congress to require those two agencies, as well as the Federal Reserve Board and all of the nation's securities exchanges, to develop a crisis plan within 60 days in an effort to help restore confidence in the markets.

A second, even more definitive report on the stock market crash was the one submitted by the President's Commission on Market Mechanisms, the so-called "Brady Report." The facts in the Brady report are compelling. A handful of the nation's largest institutional investors—employing two types of computerized trading, portfolio insurance, and stock index arbitrage—were responsible for the October stock market collapse.

Portfolio insurance is a computer-trading strategy used by institutional investors to protect profits or to offset losses in their stock holdings. In stock index arbitrage, computers gauge and trade on tiny discrepancies between stock index futures, which represent a basket of stocks, and the stocks themselves. With both techniques, computers can generate trades that will result in orders to sell huge amounts of stock in a very short period of time. What happened in all probability was that a bull market correction that began in late August (as it became apparent that the Federal Reserve was tightening credit and narrowing the supply of money), suddenly became an uncontrollable, full-fledged financial panic in part due to these computerized trading programs.

The volatility that usually accompanies a bear market is illustrated by large, 1-day percentage drops of the Dow Average. In recent years, there have been ten 1-day drops in price of 3 percent or more. Eight of those big days occurred in the fall of 1987 as noted below:

LARGEST DROPS OF DJIA

Date	Close	Decline	% Change
Oct. 19, 1987	1738.74	508.00	− 22.61%
Oct. 26, 1987	1793.93	156.83	− 8.04
Oct. 16, 1987	2246.74	108.35	− 4.60
Oct. 14, 1987	2412.70	95.46	− 3.81
Oct. 6, 1987	2548.63	91.55	− 3.47
Sept. 11, 1986	1792.89	86.61	− 4.61
Oct. 22, 1987	1950.43	77.42	− 3.82
Nov. 30, 1987	1833.55	76.93	− 4.03
July 7, 1987	1839.00	61.87	− 3.25
Nov. 9, 1987	1900.20	58.85	− 3.00

One important fact that is often overlooked is that the Dow's 5-year bull market run from August 1982 (when it stood at 777 points), to its peak in August 1987 (at 2722) was more than a *250-percent* gain. Although a 22.6-percent, 1-day drop was unprecedented, it represented a loss of only *one-fifth* of the total 5-year gain. This means that many long-term investors retained substantial gains, even after that terrible week in October.

A further lesson: 1987 was much different than 1929. There was no repeat after 1987 of the financial collapse that followed the 1929 crash because of a stronger and more alert Federal Reserve, the separation of the banking system from the market system, tougher restrictions on margin trading (buying stocks on credit), and the "safety net" of bank deposit and securities account insurance. Each of these is a result of lessons learned from 1929.

In summary, Black Monday occurred because of:

- Massive federal budget and trade deficits, which have turned the U.S. into the world's largest debtor nation.

- Sophistication of global financial markets, with computerized trading and new instruments such as stock index trading that increase market volatility.

- Negative investor psychology that translated the above factors plus lack of action from the federal government into a panicked stampede.

A stock market plunge, such as Black Tuesday of 1929 or its bigger brother Black Monday of 1987, simply reinforces one of the basic truths of stock investing: what goes up can come down. This fact makes investing in stocks highly rewarding, but highly risky as well. And while there was a Black Monday on October 19, 1987, the sun did rise (confounding some predictions), and so did the market, on Tuesday, October 20, 1987! Finally, remember that the market began to recover in November and December of 1987, with the many growth stocks snapping back in price.

But the recovery was mixed, underlining another lesson for the future: stocks that were strong before a market collapse are usually the first to come back in a market rally. For example, medium-sized, capitalized companies (those with market values of $75 to $150 million that make up the lower marginal limit for institutional investors) plunged 50 to 60 percent in the market crash of October, 1987. Among the weaker stocks, the market comeback was almost nonexistent for some months.

This was particularly true for the smaller stocks that took a severe beating in the October 1987 market collapse. They recovered much more slowly than the larger blue chips. Relatively speaking, these stocks possessed much more "value" than their larger counterparts. Further, pension funds had poured hundreds of billions of dollars into funds representing indexes of large stocks throughout the 1982–1987 bull market, overlooking the smaller stocks and thereby creating a great market inefficiency and the opportunity to buy small growth stocks cheaply.

By definition, nonblue-chip, or secondary, stocks are those stocks in a company whose market value is less than $500 million. People usually associate secondary stocks with the over-the-counter market, but nearly all of the stocks on the American Stock Exchange and some stocks on the New York Stock Exchange are also secondaries. Thus, the October plunge set the stage for a period of substantial price performance—an event that was not long in coming. Just in the month of January 1988, smaller companies measured by the NASDAQ Composite Index outperformed larger companies (measured by the Dow Jones Industrial Average) for the first time since 1983 by a margin of more than 40 percent.

This emphasizes another lesson: Selectivity, rather than blind or meaningless diversification in choosing stocks, is always the way to stock market success.

ANTICIPATING A BEAR MARKET

Is there a way to anticipate and avoid a bear market? Are there signs, either economic or financial, that experts use to perceive a market downturn? Let's look at the experts' recent record regarding the anticipation of the market crash of 1987.

At the beginning of 1986, the popular stock market forecaster Joe Granville, publisher of the *Granville Market Letter,* was unequivocal in his projection for the market. When asked what he would do with $10,000 in January of 1986, he said, "I give the current bull market only another 30 days, so I would put that $10,000 in either 90-day Treasury bills, a no load Ginnie Mae fund, or a tax-exempt bond fund. There will be a bear market for stocks by February [1986], so I suggest investing for safety with a capital 'S'."

On January 1, 1986, the Dow Jones Industrial Average stood at 1546.67. It was to soar to an all-time high of 2722.42 in August of 1987. Joe Granville was more than 18 months early in predicting that the market had reached its top!

Consider this comment by Irwin Kellner, Chief Economist at Manufacturers Hanover Trust in New York, in an interview in early 1986: "The only time stocks have continued to rise during the fourth year of an economic recovery has been in wartime." No bull's-eye for Dr. Kellner, since we ended up having a rising stock market in 1986 as well as a rising economy!

As you see, no one economist or stock market observer can consistently call the market's ups and downs. Sure, some do, once. That's pure chance. They rarely repeat. For a while, we had Joe Granville, then Robert Prechter with his Elliott Wave Theory, and, in the summer of 1987, Elaine Garzarelli of Shearson correctly calling the market's direction. But each was right only once.

The lessons drawn from past bear markets—the violent stock market storms of 1929, 1962, or 1973—would not have helped in the summer of 1987. Each one of these market declines had a different ruling characteristic that introduced a new bearish element unperceived at the time. Investors learn not to make the same mistake twice, but unfortunately, they do make different mistakes each time.

The ruling characteristic of the 1987 bear market was the sudden reality of a truly global, electronically linked stock market with an

Elaine Garzarelli of Shearson Lehman, who correctly predicted the market's direction in the summer of 1987.

amazing amount of computer-driven volatility. It was a market in which one stock exchange (Hong Kong) took extreme measures to moderate volatility by temporarily closing, and in which another, the German Stock Exchange (Frankfurt), dropped further than the New York Stock Exchange. The German market crash occurred despite its lack of the same types of economic problems that faced the U.S.

Simply put, it is hard to learn any lessons from prior bear markets that would allow us to anticipate future declines. Each down market is signaled by a series of new indicators or warning signs. There is always a search on for new signs or indicators that would help in identifying a tiring bull market or an ending bear market.

Despite the fact that each bear market has had a different set of indicators that remained unnoticed at the time but became detectable in hindsight, there are some standard indicators that often prove useful in assessing an overpriced or underpriced equity market. Valuation measures of two types—dividend yields and price earnings ratios— are often helpful (but never foolproof) in gauging a market. For instance, dividend yields on the Dow or the S & P 500 have risen to an average of 5.8 percent at bear market bottoms.

But that "average" covers a wide range of stock yields at the market lows: from 3.94 percent to 9.8 percent! For example, on the day after the crash of October 19, 1987, the Dow's dividend yield was 3.96 percent—very close to that of the bear markets of 1962 (3.94 percent) and 1966 (4 percent). So when the market is approaching a 4 percent yield, you should be cautious; in a 5 percent yield environment, you should be wildly bullish!

Another indicator that points to a bottoming of the stock market, particularly with respect to smaller emerging growth stocks, is the T. Rowe Price New Horizons Fund's price earnings ratio compared to the P/E ratio of the market as a whole. This Fund specializes in smaller growth stocks and has the longest mutual fund history of investing in them.

Generally, the average price earnings ratio of the stocks in its portfolios is much higher than the average price earnings ratio of the Standard & Poor's 500. The main reason for this difference is that there's faster growth in the earnings of the smaller companies that make up the Fund. Accordingly, when the New Horizons Fund's P/E is equal to or below that of the S & P 500, smaller growth stocks are usually an outstanding buy. That statistical relationship has happened twice since the Fund was started in 1961—once in 1977, just prior to the historic rise in growth stock prices that peaked in 1983, and again in the late fall of 1987 when, after 5 years of underperformance, smaller growth companies began to do well.

There is considerable logic behind this P/E indicator; fear, uncertainty, and despair drive the prices of these smaller companies down much more rapidly than the prices of bigger and more capitalized growth stocks, because the smaller stocks have low or nonexistent dividends. The more capitalized stocks provide dividend yields that normally cushion a stock's fall. Typically, a smaller growth company needs all the capital it can get, so all or most of the earnings are reinvested back into the business.

Even these two indicators don't supply the answer to coping with a bear market. Indicators can be helpful, but you shouldn't bet your portfolio on them. Nevertheless, some super stock investors may feel more comfortable if they're able to monitor the market's health. To complement the two "bottom" indicators previously detailed, here are five signals of a stock market "top":

1). Heavy selling by corporate insiders. When there are five insiders selling for every one buying, it becomes unnerving. Insiders are the most knowledgeable investors around.

2). Low cash reserves among institutional investors. The reserves level becomes critical when cash in mutual funds drops to 6 or 7 percent of total assets and pension-fund cash percentages drop into the single digits, indicating that the funds don't have any more cash to put into stocks.

3). A sharp increase in inflation and interest rates, heralded by soaring commodity prices. When commodity prices go through the roof, inflation follows, and then interest rates go up and stocks start to collapse. When investors find they can get a better return in money market funds or bonds, they'll sell off stocks, pushing down stock prices.

4). Heavy participation by individual investors in the market. Despite the explosive growth of mutual funds during the 1980s, most of the real gains were in long-term bond funds. Watch for individuals getting swept up in a speculative fervor for stocks. When *everyone* is talking about investing in stocks, it's a sign that the market is getting somewhere near its end.

5). A broad-based sell-off of stocks accompanied by heavy trading volume. This indicates that many investors might be taking their profits and getting out of the stock market.

Watch for these signals but also keep your perspective. Remember that in the long run, stock selectivity is more important than calling turns in the stock market's direction.

More important than indicators or signals are the lessons of experience. Survival can be learned best from seasoned investors— those who have successfully weathered a number of down markets. They all advise the same things: *Don't try to time the market, buy for the long term, and only invest with money you can afford to lose.*

Focus on those companies with good records and equally good prospects, and don't sell a stock unless the company changes dramatically or unless you need the money. Frequent selling and buying does provide a certain amount of excitement or glamour, but it also puts an emotional burden on your decision-making processes. Once you're out of the market, it may be psychologically difficult to turn that cash around and buy back in again. And remember that the brokerage commissions on all those transactions can add up and take a sizable chunk out of your net gain.

The people who held steady during the 1973–1974 bear market saw their stocks go down, but then they watched those same stocks move to new highs several years later. "Buy and hold" might not be glamorous and exciting, but it *is* the one successful technique that anyone can use to prosper!

One way to handle a severe decline in stock prices calmly is to view investing in the stock market the same way you would shopping in a large department store. Let's say you want to buy a Persian rug. You price it at a department store such as Bloomingdale's for $5,000. Several weeks later, you spot the same rug again, and this time the price is marked down by 20 percent to $4,000. You decide it's really attractive now, and so you buy it.

A month later, you see the same rug advertised in the paper for $3,000—that's a 40-percent discount on the original price and $1,000 cheaper than what you paid. You feel terrible, and somewhat defeated. Tell yourself that you *did* buy at less than full price and that you are enjoying a good product. (Think of how badly those who purchased it at $5,000 feel!) You might even consider buying a second rug for $3,000 since it is the bargain of a lifetime!

Stocks aren't much different from those rugs. Stocks are marked down and then are marked back up as their value becomes more apparent—just like Persian rugs. The difference is that when stocks are discounted by 25 to 30 percent, no one wants to buy them until someone else buys first! That's the psychology of fear at work.

The prices prevailing in the stock market or a particular stock's price are not always good indicators of the company's progress or worth. You should gauge when and if to buy a stock based on the company's sales, profits, and financial strength. Obviously, the trick is always to be sure that you don't pay more than a stock is worth. But when a stock's price drops not because of its sales or earnings but simply because of market psychology, you shouldn't berate yourself because you didn't get it at the "best" price (remember Bloomingdale's and our rugs). Instead, realize that you are getting a unique opportunity to buy more high-quality merchandise at an even lower price!

Making long-term investments in stocks with strong earnings momentum was one of the hallmarks of the T. Rowe Price Growth Stock Fund, a star performer of the 1950s and 1960s. One of Mr. Price's more brilliant acquisitions was stock in IBM. He first bought IBM in 1950 for $5 a share. By 1987, the same stock was selling at $116 a share. This Fund is proof that even if you can't guess the direction of the stock market, if your selections are good growth stocks, you'll make money anyway!

THE END OF A BEAR MARKET

When you are in a bear market, the first thing to think about is when it will turn around. You want to be sure you get in on the ground floor of the next bull market.

Sensing the end of a bear market is difficult, since rational price behavior in the stock market becomes rare or nonexistent. The causes of bear markets are usually more psychological than financial.

As a market begins to plunge downward, most investors become increasingly frightened by widening losses. High levels of emotion and extreme pessimism are easier to see than low price earnings ratios and high dividend yields.

After a market crash of substantial proportions, there will usually be a reflex rally of stock prices coming off an extreme devaluation. Eventually, though, that rally loses momentum as more and more investors are eager to sell at high prices. This slows and then ends the rally, and the market sinks to its previous, post-crash low or even exceeds it. Months might go by before any real improvement in overall prices is experienced.

If there is one thing that characterizes a bear market, it is that completion of a bottom in stock prices takes time—a lot of time. Confidence has been shaken, and substantial amounts of money have flowed out of stocks into bonds and money market funds. It takes time to reverse that flow.

Part of the "bottoming out process" can be recognized in the bad news on stock brokerage firms—the layoff of personnel, accompanied by increasing bankruptcies and generally negative articles about the state of the brokerage industry. This is the result of a lack of investor interest; trading volume slows down as both the public and institutions ignore stocks. Bear markets in the process of "bottoming" are dull and have little price activity.

Equity investment is almost completely rejected, and only the gradual improvement of statistic after statistic will lure both new and experienced investors back into the market again. That first movement usually begins with rising prices in investment-grade stocks, particularly defensive stocks like utilities. The reason is that at this point, while an increasing number of market experts are gradually becoming "bullish," institutions and money managers are still capital-preservation-oriented and therefore don't want to risk their money in volatile issues. This results in a drive toward quality issues.

Two other events that herald the end of a bear market are: the Dow Jones Industrial Average rising above its 200-day moving average line, and then, the number of advances (stocks whose prices have risen over the last day or week) steadily overtaking the number of declines (those whose prices have fallen over the same time period). This improvement will be slow, almost undetectable at first. Watching for a bear market to end and taking advantage of it takes patience, but then so does almost anything worthwhile!

*Failure isn't what hurts you . . .
it's the fear of failure that does the
damage.*

Actor JACK LEMMON
in a television interview (1988)

8

The Chicken Investor

ONE OF THE WORST FEARS INVESTORS HAVE IS FEAR OF BUYING A PO-
tential super stock at the market high. And it's not an unreasonable
fear, since individual stock prices are related more to the general market
direction than to any other factor.

MARKET TIMING

Buying even the best potential super stock at the wrong time in
the market would hurt your overall investment performance. You could
be correct on your stock selection, but still invest badly by buying the
right stock at the wrong time in the stock market. Is it possible to
avoid this? Not really, although there are some guidelines you can use
to gauge whether the stock market is being overbought or oversold.
But doesn't the volatility of the stock market itself make it more
important to determine *when* to buy rather than *what* to buy?

The answer would be "yes" if you could time the market well
enough to buy at or near the market's bottom and sell at or near its
top. And that's extremely difficult, if not impossible. There's an old

saying on Wall Street: "Nobody rings a bell at the top (or the bottom) of a market." In other words, none of those famous indicators you hear about really clue investors to get out of a bull market near the top or into one at the bottom.

Nonetheless, each time the stock market experiences a big decline, we hear about those shrewd people who sold smart. More likely they were just lucky. But once they've sold, these experts will not be successful unless they get back into stocks near the market low (whenever that occurs) in order to benefit from the next rise. History, as documented by a number of thorough academic studies, shows that this is extremely hard to do.

There are some basic reasons why successful market timing is so difficult. First, as I have mentioned, major turns in stock prices are usually triggered by unpredictable events. Second, it is hard to be bearish (and sell) when the consensus is strongly bullish, and it is extremely hard to be bullish when virtually everyone else is bearish.

Third, while you should sell individual stocks that are clearly overpriced, selling "the market" and going heavily into cash involves swimming against the tide. The history of American stock prices since World War II reflects a long-term uptrend in prices—with major fluctuations, of course, above and below the trend line. As the U.S. economy has grown, earnings and dividends have trended upward, along with interim fluctuations.

Being "out of the market" works extremely well at certain times, but in the past 4 decades, stocks have risen in 26 years, been about even in 3 years, and declined in only 11 years. So the odds of being successful when you're heavily in cash are almost three to one against you.

ADVANTAGES OF LONG-TERM INVESTMENT

A study of stocks and the stock market, completed in 1988 by Professors Richard Woodward and Jess Chua (of the University of Calgary), shows that holding stocks as long-term investments works much better than market timing. This was the result of gains in bull markets more than making up for losses in bear markets. They conclude that a market timer would have to make correct decisions 70 percent of the time to do better than the buy-and-hold, long-term investor. Being right 70 percent of the time in predicting market turns has to

The Long-Term Trend in Stock Prices

S & P 500 Stock Index—Percent Change in Principal Value
June 30, 1949 Through October 19, 1987

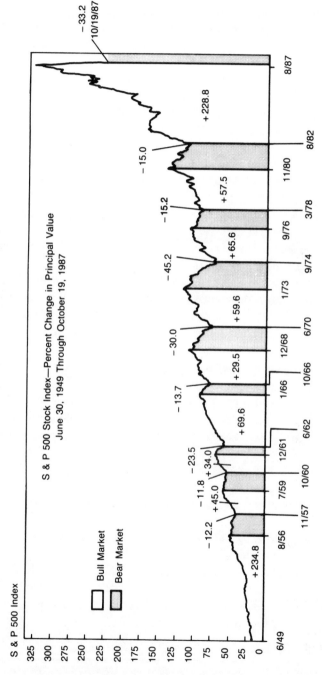

be nearly impossible. A further bar to timing success lies in excessive transactions costs, or commissions paid to move in and out of stocks.

Happily, it is not necessary to get out of a bull market in preparation for a bear market. If you have the right stock then—even if you bought it at the top of a bull market—you will come through a bear market surprisingly well. We've demonstrated that no one can consistently forecast the stock market's direction short term. The right or wrong time will only be perceived by looking back. Hindsight is a wonderful thing!

But even if you bought your stock at the wrong time, you still will do well if your selection was correct and you have *patience*. The key to being a "chicken" investor is to buy solid stocks with reliable earnings growth selectively, and to have patience. If you do this, eventually time will take care of the problem of a bear market.

Let's take the worse possible case in order to illustrate the triumph of selectivity and patience. Instead of using an example stock, we will use the Dow Jones Industrial Average as our "stock"—hardly a thoroughbred racer of the super stock type. Even though it's not a super stock, this average index investment is still a good example of how buying at the high point in the market will not be fatal to your long-run investment strategy. Further, let's assume that we bought shares of that large bundle of Dow stocks at the highest point in the market in 1929, just before the crash. We made equal dollar investments in the Dow average each year from 1929 through 1966. We'll make the scenario even worse. Assume that we purchased those Dow stocks at their highest price not only in 1929 but in each year since then!

This "strategy" of buying the Dow at its yearly high worked badly for the first few years as the market continued to plummet. Nevertheless, during the terrible years of 1930, 1931, 1932, and 1933, those fixed dollars were buying large numbers of shares at extremely low prices.

Consequently, by 1935, the portfolio was beginning to show a profit. Twenty-five years later, the Dow Jones Industrial Average had finally worked its way back to its 1929 peak, and the portfolio of buying fixed dollar amounts of stocks each year had more than doubled in value! By 1966, the Dow Jones Industrial Average was 161 percent above its 1929 level. Compare that to the performance of our program of buying the Dow Average each year with a fixed dollar amount (also known as dollar cost averaging). Our gain was 336 percent over cost!

Even in the bull and bear markets of the late 1960s, 1973 to 1974, and all of the markets through the bear market low in 1982, you could have bought the Dow at each year's high and still made money. Not only does this system work for the staid Dow Jones Industrial Average, it works for individual stocks too; and it works even better for super stocks.

Here is a small list of super stocks bought at the wrong time (at their high for the year) and how they have fared subsequently:

Company	Business	Highest/ Lowest Price 1982	Highest/ Lowest Price 1987
1. Circuit City Stores	Retailer	1½-¾	34¼-11¾
2. Community Psychiatric	Acute Care	11-5	32-18
3. Merck	Drugs	44-32	223-122
4. Toys 'R' Us	Discount Toy Stores	16-5	42-22
5. Wal-Mart Stores	Retailer	6-2	42-20

As the tabulation indicates, you could have bought Wal-Mart Stores stock at an adjusted price of $6 a share in 1982, only to watch in dismay as it dropped to a low of $2 in the very same year. Yet by 1987 that same stock, sold at $42 a share at the high and even the "crash" low of $20 a share, was still significantly above the original purchase price.

Another good example is Merck. You would have bought Merck at a high of $44 in 1982 and again watched as it dropped to $32 in the bear market of that year. If you had held on, by 1987 that same stock sold at a high of $223. Even the low in the 1987 bear market was comfortably ahead of the purchase price of 4 and a half years ago. The point is: *Patience and selectivity are the secret weapons of the "chicken investor."*

EMOTIONAL SURVIVAL IN DOWN MARKETS

We have often heard the view that the shortsightedness of American business—the attention paid to quarter-by-quarter results rather than long-term economic planning—is to blame for many of our industrial problems in the U.S. This disdain of long-range planning (not

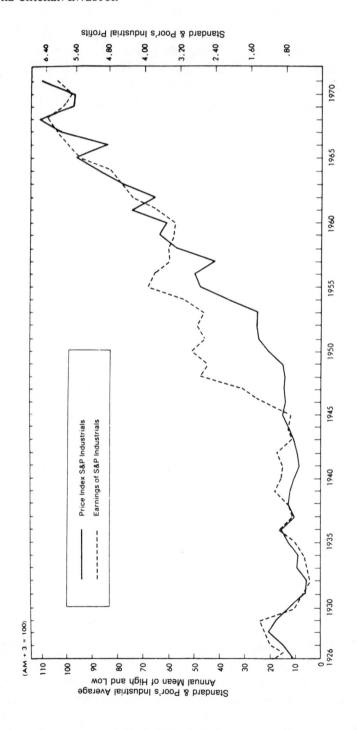

The Long-Term Tie Between Earnings and Stock Prices
1926-1971

Source: Standard & Poor's
*Based on 425 stocks.

shared by the Japanese corporate officers) has been a major factor in the decline of American competitiveness.

A similar conclusion can be drawn about the lack of success of most investors in the stock market. Indeed, most investors, both institutional and individual, are too narrow-minded. An increasing number of studies demonstrates that most investors wrongly focus on current profit results rather than watching future earnings. To gauge future earnings, all one has to do is observe stock performance and reports of current earnings; there is a strong positive association with reported earnings.

The dramatic response by investors to quarter-to-quarter fluctuations in earnings is matched by company management's fixation on short-term performance. Certainly, each group's actions affects the other in a deadly, closed circuit. Add to this both media focus and the federal government's fondness for monthly economic statistics, and that's the recipe for confusion and volatility in the stock market. It is hard to maintain perspective amid all this hoopla. But excessive concentration on the short term might be injurious to your investment health!

Nevertheless, there will be some investors who still have a problem with the "patience factor." They know that it might take years for their investment to pay off, and during those years, they'll feel they could be doing something more productive with their money. For them, there are other techniques for coping with the price swings of a bull or bear market.

Fear of loss, coupled with the despair of not being able to anticipate the rise or fall of market prices (and the fluctuations of a specific stock) may skew the decision-making process of even the most knowledgeable and stable of investors. Don't let panic be an excuse for inaction. There are several methods that will help a chicken investor minimize risk and/or make the risk more palatable. Four of the most effective things you can do are: (1) Diversify your assets; (2) Use convertible securities when possible; (3) Consider dollar cost averaging; and (4) Buy only with cash, never with credit.

Diversification of Assets

Diversification of assets is such a simple concept that most advisors assume it is implicit in all investment thinking and, consequently, not worth mentioning. Nevertheless, diversification remains the single most important step you can take to insulate yourself from stock market ups and downs.

The technique in diversification is to divide your investment among various different asset types—not only stocks, but bonds, real estate, and perhaps some gold. Each of these assets has a different investment cycle. For instance, when stocks go down in a panic, gold goes up. In a boom period, stocks will move up vigorously while bonds will decline, and so on.

How much should be apportioned to each category depends on your age and current financial condition, but the general rule is: the younger you are, the more long-term your investment can be, and, consequently, you will be able to assume greater risks.

Asset diversification assures you that in any investment climate you will make money—even in a bear market. That very fact allows you peace of mind and contributes to your sense of objectivity so that you can pursue a long-term strategy.

Benefits of Convertible Securities

Whenever there is a high degree of concern regarding the stock market trend, such as a bear market or even a bull market that appears to be overvalued and speculative, the question becomes: Should I buy bonds and play it safe? If I do, will I miss out on the next market rise?

Suppose there was a conservative investment that could turn into a super stock at any time, gave a good yield, and had an upside profit potential, a limited downside risk, and a commission cost 50 percent lower than that of stocks. Would you be interested? The answer is obviously "yes." And such features are precisely what a convertible security can offer.

When equity markets are more volatile, and CD's and money market funds are paying attractive yields, convertibles make sense. When you identify a super stock that you want to buy, check to see if the company has a convertible security—one that is convertible into common stock. Convertibles can work to protect you on the downside, yet still give you a substantial play on the rise of the common stock.

A convertible security (it can be a bond or a preferred stock issue) gives you the right to exchange that security for a specific number of common shares of stock at a later date, and, meanwhile, pays a fixed rate of return. If the convertible is a bond, the return is in the form of semiannual interest payments. In the case of convertible preferred stock, the return is paid as quarterly dividends.

Because of their fixed return rates, the price of convertibles tends to rise or fall as interest rates rise or fall. Since the convertible can be exchanged for common stock, it offers you the potential for profit should the price of common stock rise, providing protection in a bear market. Convertibles have downside buffer similar to that of a straight bond or preferred stock because their income is higher than that of the company's underlying common stock. One extra benefit is that falling or low interest rates—typical in the latter stages of a bear market—can also enhance a convertible bond's value.

Why more conservative investors do not invest in the convertible market continues to be a mystery. Commissions on convertibles, particularly bonds, are usually significantly less than the commissions on stock sales. For you, that means a savings in both your purchase and selling costs.

Also, convertible preferred stock normally provides double or triple the modest yields produced by common stock. In fact, when the common stock is growing fast, there might be no dividend at all, since all of the profits are being pumped back into the company to keep up the pace of growth. So you can see, convertibles allow you to participate in the upward move of a stock but also help to cushion your fall in a down market.

To gauge a convertible bond's attractiveness, simply calculate what a bond costs in relation to the company's underlying stock. If the cost of the stock is less than 15 percent more than the convertible's price, then you probably have a very attractive value—20 percent is normal and over 30 percent is too high.

In addition, keep in mind that if the market does not perform the way you expected, convertible bonds historically never go down in price (percentage-wise) as much as the underlying stock. The convertible bond on the way down acts exactly as a bond; and on the way up, it acts as a stock. When the market is down, the interest yield on the bond will cushion the fall; when the market is up, the bond has a conversion price to the underlying stock, which is in direct relation to the price of the stock. In addition, you get an annual yield that, in most cases, is comparable to what you can get in money market mutual funds or short term CD's.

Dollar Cost Averaging—The Hidden Investment

Dollar cost averaging is a strategy that allows you to survive a bear market and gives you superior investment performance. But you must follow the strategy to the letter. A glimpse of the effectiveness of this program was offered in the previous example of buying the Dow Jones averages during the Depression and afterward. This system works because it beats the market by ignoring the market!

"Beating the market," or exceeding the Standard and Poor's 500 Average or the Dow Jones Industrial Average, is a reflection of superior market performance; and yet many investors, including a large number of professionals, fail to do so. The reason is in the definition of the term "average." Over any given period, about half of all investors *must* do worse than the market average, arithmetically. Among these will be professionals as well as amateurs. Accordingly, surpassing the market averages is difficult, but not impossible to do.

Dollar cost averaging is simply the systematic purchase of a single stock in fixed dollar amounts at regular time intervals regardless of fluctuations in the stock's price. For example, you could invest $1,000 in the stock every 3 months. Or $100 every month. Or $500 every week. The amount and frequency of your investments depends upon your financial resources.

Once you begin dollar cost averaging, it is crucial to the success of the program that you stay on track. Never miss an investment or reduce its dollar amount. With this in mind, set up an investment schedule you're sure you can afford. In a real sense, dollar cost averaging is cost averaging—a type of "forced" savings plan. It ignores all market fluctuations. Will such a basic system beat the market? The answer is yes!

The way dollar cost averaging works can be best illustrated with a simple example. Let's assume you have decided to invest $1,000 in Alpha Company stock every 6 months. In the beginning, the shares sell for $10. Therefore, you open an account and buy 100 shares at $10 each with your first $1,000. When it's time for your next investment, 6 months later, the overall market has climbed, and Alpha is selling for $20 a share.

You then buy 50 shares at $20 each, for another investment of $1,000. Two months later, the market has corrected some of its advance, and Alpha's price has fallen back to $15, the average of your $10 and $20 purchases. At this point, you break even, right? Wrong!

You've really made a nice profit! Your $2,000 total investment bought you 150 shares total. Those 150 shares times their current value of $15 is worth $2,250. That's about a 12 percent profit over your $2,000 cost!

Your superior return occurred because your fixed dollar investment bought relatively more shares when the price was low and relatively fewer shares when the price was high. The arithmetic is simple:

1st Buy	- 100 shares @ $10 per share =	$1,000
2nd Buy	- 50 shares @ $20 per share =	1,000
Total:	150 shares	$2,000

and
Average cost per share ($2,000 divided by 150) = $13.33

Now that the stock is selling at $15, you obviously have a profit ($250 total, or $1.67 per share). Also observe that the average transaction price, $15, is more than our real average cost per share of only $13.33. This astounding result will always hold true with dollar cost averaging. Because you invest a fixed dollar amount each time, you always buy a larger number of shares when the price is lower and a smaller number of shares when the price is higher. In effect, you are buying a lot at bargain prices and relatively little at what might be considered exorbitantly high prices.

There is a risk in dollar cost averaging. Only in retrospect will we know which prices really were bargains and which prices were too high. While a few stocks will move further up or down than others, the prices of most company shares will move with the trend of the stock market.

Nevertheless, over longer periods of time, nearly all stocks will tend to follow the course of the market to some extent. Since you may end up averaging on a stock that continues to go down rather than fluctuate, it is essential that you pick a stock that will eventually recover in value over time. Put another way, you should never dollar-average a stock that eventually goes into bankruptcy. There are two ways to minimize the risk of this happening. One is to use investigation and analysis to assure yourself that your stock (company) has not only potential growth but also business staying power. The super stock "scorecard" will be of considerable help in doing this.

But even that might not be enough. The second way to reduce the risk of a mistake is to diversify. Select several of the most promising stocks to dollar-average. At least three and ideally five stocks should be included in a dollar-cost-averaged portfolio. With the purchase of multiple stock issues, you gain additional insurance against a significant decline in any one stock affecting your super stock portfolio's performance.

Another benefit of dollar cost averaging is that it reduces your portfolio risk. Historical studies show that in order to reduce risk and maximize investment returns, you should buy and hold securities over long time periods. The diversification resulting from buying stocks over time reduces risk more effectively than the traditional diversification method of buying many different stocks. Since dollar cost averaging is pure time diversification, it not only works to improve your returns, it also reduces your total portfolio risk.

One of the disciplines you must exercise before you can bank on the benefits of dollar averaging is to ignore all market fluctuations. The principal failure of most investors is that they allow their emotions to rule their decision-making. When stock prices are rising and everyone is bullish, emotional investors will buy, and then when the market is falling, they become frightened and sell, hoping to buy back again later at an even lower price. This rarely works. No one can consistently forecast the market, and few investors know how to take advantage of a market decline, even if they do see one coming before it gets there.

The beauty of the dollar-cost-averaging strategy is that you can ignore the ups and downs of both the stock market and your individual stock(s). As a matter of fact, "down" or bear markets—when everyone else is fearful and selling off stocks—become your opportunity for enhanced success, since you are buying more shares at a lower price. The reverse is also true: In a bull market—when everyone is buying— you are buying fewer shares at those high prices. In effect, dollar cost averagers allow the system to do their market timing for them!

The investing intervals for dollar cost averaging are also important. You can make your investments as often as you wish: weekly, monthly, or even annually. However, the more frequent your investments, the better the results. Since stocks can quickly swing violently up or down, it is important for the average that you buy a large number of shares with your fixed-dollar investment when the market is at a low.

But a market low might not occur at the time you are scheduled to make an investment. Accordingly, the more frequently your program calls for reinvestment, the closer the program will come to enabling you to buy shares at the precise low of an intermediate or major market downtrend. As you can see, dollar cost averaging almost makes you *hope* that prices will go down, so that you can buy more shares and build up your portfolio!

Investors often hesitate to start a dollar-cost-averaging program because they believe the market is "too high" at the moment. They plan instead to sit it out and wait for a market decline before beginning their purchases. Although this may at first sound wise, no one really knows when the market (or a stock) is "too high." Only when looking back can we truly gauge an overvaluation, so it's best to start dollar cost averaging as soon as you're financially able to start "beating" the market simply by ignoring it!

Buy With Cash—Not Credit

The last advice I have for surviving a bear market is to buy your super stocks with cash. Don't ever use credit or margin your stocks to make purchases. Borrowing *can* give you big gains if stocks go up; that's called the power of leverage. However, if before your stock begins to move, it goes down even slightly, you'll have a big problem.

In a typical margin credit arrangement, an investor puts up 50 percent of the market price of the stock and the brokerage house finances a loan for the rest. If your stock goes down in value, you will have to put up still more money or stock as collateral to meet that 50-percent requirement. Most firms require that you maintain collateral in your account that exceeds your margin loan by at least 30 percent of the market value of the stock(s). Interest charges are usually several percentage points above the prime rate, so just maintaining such an account can be costly. The results if your stock fails to go up will be severe, and if your stock goes down, you'll lose money you don't even have. Never, *ever* use a margin account. They're just too dangerous.

WHEN TO SELL

Ideally, the answer to the question of when to sell would be "never." This would imply that your stock selection is perfect; earnings per share and sales are always on track, declines in the stock are never more than 15 percent, and everything goes along beautifully! Unfortunately this is rarely the case, and you must anticipate that dreaded day when you might have to sell. Learning how to sell is infinitely more difficult than learning how to buy.

It's easy to fall in love with a stock. You like its higher-than-usual growth rate, it has a solid financial structure, and it's reasonably priced in relation to its potential. So you buy it, and it works. A year or so later, the stock is 30-percent or 40-percent higher in price. You begin to wonder whether you should take the gain and go elsewhere. What do you do?

Even the greatest growth stock of the 1960s and early 1970s, Xerox Corporation, had to be sold at some point. It was the most glamorous of the growth stocks, and it had doubled, redoubled, and doubled again, making hundreds of its early stockholders rich. By 1973, the stock sold at a high of $173 a share. Yet, that same stock sold at only $50 a share in the October bear market of 1987, and, even in the spring of 1988, it had barely recovered to $61. Somewhere between 1973 and 1988, Xerox stock should have been sold and the money employed elsewhere. But how would you have known when to sell?

In the case of Xerox, its share price lagged so much that its dividend yield grew to 5 percent—an amazing figure for a growth stock—but by then, Xerox was no longer a growth stock. Because of severe price competition from Japanese copiers in the 1970s, Xerox tried to build its earnings by going beyond its original copier franchise. The company stumbled time and time again, diversifying into minicomputers, word processors, typewriters, and facsimile transmission machines, all with little or no success. Even its financial services investment, an insurance company, yielded lower-than-expected returns when the property casualty business turned down.

Somewhere along the line, fundamental or industry indicators should have pointed to the sale of Xerox stock. Which indicators should an investor look for? There are no hard-and-fast rules for selling, but there are some points to consider.

First. Whenever a stock makes up more than 10 percent of your portfolio, you should cut back that holding no matter how "rosy" its outlook may be. This is simple and prudent diversification. It never makes sense to increase your risk by overconcentration in one stock.

Second. Don't be in a hurry to sell a stock just because you think it is too high. Stocks that seem "too high" have a frustrating tendency to move even higher. If you want to protect your profits while still participating in the continued upward move, then give your broker a "stop loss order," which instructs him to sell your holdings in the stock if it declines by more than the percentage you have specified (10 to 15 percent is typical).

Here's how it works: Say you buy a stock at $10 a share, and it rises to $20. In order to protect your profit but still retain the possibility of gaining even more if the stock's price continues to rise, you hold the stock but issue a "stop loss order," telling your broker to sell the stock if it falls below a certain point—for our example, $17.

You should select a stop order price that is sufficiently below the current price to insulate you from short-term fluctuations but still high enough to protect most of the profit you've already made on it. If the stock sinks to $17, your stop order automatically becomes an order to sell, or "market order."

There is one catch, however. Just because you've ordered the stock to be sold if it reaches $17 doesn't necessarily mean someone will buy it at $17. All it means is that you will automatically be sold out at the best price available the day it hits $17, which could be a lot less than $17 if the stock (or the market itself) takes a big dive that day.

Stop orders can also be done on a "trailing" basis. Say, for example, your stock goes from $20 to $30. At $30, you institute a stop order at $27 (a 10-percent stop order). If the stock then goes up to $34, you cancel the $27 stop order and replace it with a new 10-percent stop order at $30 ½.

Stop orders can be limited to a day-, week-, or month-long period, or issued "good until cancelled." When executed between dealers on the New York or American Stock Exchange, stop orders are handled electronically; but for OTC stocks, a broker must execute the trade manually, which takes much longer.

Legendary investor Roy Neuberger advocated always using 10-percent stop loss orders because he believed no matter how good an investor thought his judgment was, he should always give himself a 10-percent leeway for error!

Third. Consider using "limit orders" for buying and selling stock. A limit order can ensure that an investor gets at least a certain minimum price when shares are sold or that an investor pays no more than a certain price when buying a stock. For instance, a limit order to buy a stock at $20 would instruct the broker to buy only if the stock falls to $20 or below. A limit order to sell at $20 would tell the broker to

Two Examples of the Power of Compound Interest

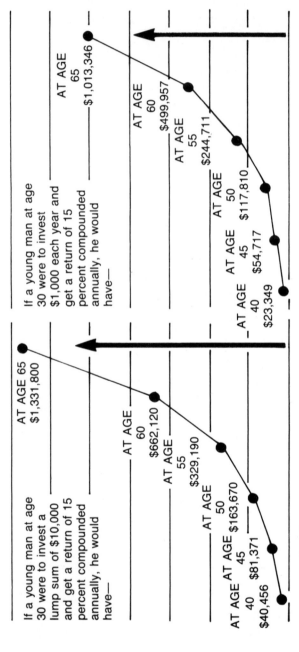

If a young man at age 30 were to invest a lump sum of $10,000 and get a return of 15 percent compounded annually, he would have—

AT AGE 40 $40,456
AT AGE 45 $81,371
AT AGE 50 $163,670
AT AGE 55 $329,190
AT AGE 60 $662,120
AT AGE 65 $1,331,800

If a young man at age 30 were to invest $1,000 each year and get a return of 15 percent compounded annually, he would have—

AT AGE 40 $23,349
AT AGE 45 $54,717
AT AGE 50 $117,810
AT AGE 55 $244,711
AT AGE 60 $499,957
AT AGE 65 $1,013,346

Note: Examples assume reinvestment of all dividends and payment from other income of taxes due on annual dividends.

sell only if he can get at least $20 per share and, otherwise, to hold.

Limit orders can make sense in volatile markets, but although they do provide price protection, they give no guarantee that your market order will be executed. For example, you tell your broker to buy ABC Corporation if it drops to $30 or less. But by the time he puts in your order, the supply of ABC stock available at $30 has been bought up by investors whose brokers got there before yours, and because of the laws of supply and demand, ABC's price has bounced back up to $31 a share and your broker is no longer authorized to buy it for you.

Fourth. Examine small holdings (less than 4 percent of your portfolio) carefully to assess their suitability. If you conclude that the stock fits your objective, then buy more. If not, sell it, and reinvest in something better. As a rule, don't invest less than 4 percent in any one industry.

Fifth. Sell off a "disappointment" stock before it's too late. Let's say you bought a stock that was supposed to grow and it hasn't. Instead, its sales and earnings have slowed. It might be time to sell if its price gains have lagged behind overall stock market gains. How long should you wait? About 2 years. If investors had used this rule on Xerox stock in the 1970s, they would have saved themselves a lot of grief.

On the other hand, if you bought a stock on the basis of growth in sales and earnings and suddenly sales drop and so do profits, you should immediately question your initial analysis. Review both the analysis and decision. In this case, how long should you wait? Two quarters of "down" sales and earnings are long enough. After that, think about selling—fast. Remember, knowing when to sell is more important than knowing when to buy!

9

Be an Analyst

COMPLETE, RELIABLE, AND UP-TO-DATE INFORMATION ABOUT COMPANies and industries is fundamental to identifying super stocks. Your decisions are only as good as your information. Useful investment information is of three types:

1). Timely and general information about the current business climate, the stock market, and individual companies.
2). Specific information about interesting industries and companies.
3). Securities and Exchange Commission (SEC) reports.

The best sources of timely and general information about business and the stock and bond markets are newspapers and magazines. Your objective should be to keep in touch with business and market trends and to develop a constantly evolving list of possibilities that then can be screened down to a few more promising super stock prospects that merit further research.

Information about specific industries and companies can be found in your public library, your brokerage house's research department, and the various financial and investment advisory services. You can also contact individual companies for information such as quarterly sales figures or an annual report.

After you have narrowed dozens of possibilities down to a few good prospects, detailed information sufficient to develop your super stock scorecard (see Chapter 5) should be obtained from company sources. Most companies will place you on their mailing lists for financial material. Be sure to request annual reports for the last 5 years and the most recent quarterly reports.

ANNUAL REPORTS

The annual report is the principal document used by companies to communicate directly with its shareholders. It usually contains both quantitative and qualitative information about the company and its operations. Each company also publishes proxy statements that provide official notification to designated classes of stockholders of matters to be brought to a vote at the next shareholders' meeting.

Proxy votes may be solicited for such decisions as changing the company name, transferring large blocks of stock, or electing new officers. Proxy statements can also announce a company change so important that the stockholders, rather than the board of directors, must vote on it. Shareholders receive proxy statements automatically, while other investors can request them from the company or find them in business libraries.

In addition to financial material, request news releases, reprints of articles published, and speeches made by management. The latter may be especially useful in providing perspective on a company, since managers usually cover a great deal of operating history when they speak before analyst groups throughout the country.

A letter addressed to the secretary of your target company requesting information will place you on its mailing list. Company addresses can be located in the business reference section of your local library. For example, most libraries carry the *Standard & Poor's Directory,* which lists companies' addresses and their officers.

SEC REPORTS

Nearly all companies whose stocks are traded publicly must file certain documents with the Securities and Exchange Commission (SEC). These reports are extensive and include a great deal of information useful to an individual investor. The most important are the 10K, 10Q, and 8K reports.

The Form 10K is an annual report on company operations, required by and filed with the SEC, that goes into much greater detail than the company's glossy annual report. The first and most important part of the 10K includes a business description, a 5-year summary of operations, a listing of properties and parent corporations and/or subsidiaries, the details of any pending legal proceedings, and the company's financial statements. The second part profiles management, its pay and benefits, and the company's principal security holders. For the purpose of basic analysis, the 10K is the most important statistical report filed with the SEC.

Form 10Q is similar to Form 10K but is filed quarterly rather than annually. Accordingly, its information is more current and useful. However the 10Q, unlike the annual 10K, is unaudited, and thus is subject to year-end adjustments.

Form 8K is useful for super stock investors because it details material changes that were considered by the SEC to be so important that they couldn't wait for publication in the next 10Q. Thus, this report outlines *unscheduled* material events or corporate changes deemed of importance to shareholders or to the SEC, including changes in control of the company's registrant, recent acquisition or disposition of assets, and bankruptcy or receivership. Any changes in the registrant's management would also be noted in an 8K, as would resignation of one or more of the registrant's directors.

Sometimes these reports are available from the reporting company. If not, copies can be obtained from the SEC by writing to:

The Securities and Exchange Commission
Washington, D.C. 20025

PERIODICALS/OTHER PUBLICATIONS

For general business information read the *Wall Street Journal* daily. The *Journal* is the daily "bible" of current investment information and will keep you apprised of all corporate and economic news.

Investor's Daily is another periodical packed with valuable data for the detail-oriented investor who uses a lot of statistics, volume-price relationships, and other technical data. It supplements the *Wall Street Journal.*

Barron's, a business and financial weekly, is less topical and more detailed than the *Journal.* Each issue contains several in-depth articles on financial, corporate, or economic subjects of interest to investors. Separate sections cover the weekly events in the stock and bond markets, commodities, options, and foreign investment. Also included are several research pieces on attractive individual stocks or sectors. Finally, *Barron's* is packed with weekly stock and bond tables, economic indicators, and other financial data. This weekly is essential for serious investors.

The Media General Financial Weekly is a newspaper delivered every Monday. It carries detailed information concerning earnings, dividends, stock prices, and volume for roughly 3400 companies, separated into industry groups. It includes every common stock listed on the NYSE and AMEX, plus about 700 OTC stocks. Each week the performance of the different industry groups is shown for the current week, and for the last 4, 13, and 52 weeks. A number of charts and tables are provided on the market indices, dividend yields, P/E ratios, volume, and so forth. Regular columns include fixed-income securities, the "market week", selected research reports and other items of current interest.

Business Week magazine, also a weekly, covers a broader business beat, including marketing and labor, as well as economy and finance. Corporate problems and successes are given extensive coverage, and such profiles can often stimulate new investment ideas.

Forbes is published biweekly and is written for the average investor. Companies, industries, and individuals are all portrayed in a readable and stimulating manner. The magazine publishes articles on various companies and investments topics, as well as columnists with opinions on particular market segments and activities. *Forbes* contains a wealth of useful economic information, including an index that measures U.S. economic activity, with graphs of its eight components (industrial production, factory orders, housing starts, etc.). It also supplies graphs of the Dow Jones Industrial Average and the Wilshire 5000 stock market index. Tables comparing six market indices for the last 4 weeks and 52 weeks and others showing stock market performance based on "five key investor yardsticks" are also included. In addition, one issue each year evaluates the performance of mutual funds.

Fortune is a biweekly magazine with articles on general business trends, written from the perspective of corporate managers. Individual investors will find the "Personal Investing" section especially interesting.

For specific information about companies and industries, visit your local library. There you will find information collected by the three major investment advisory services: *Moody's, Standard & Poor's,* and *Value Line. Moody's* manuals are a basic source of historical data, which is bound in large and complete volumes and published annually for most industrial, utility, transportation, and finance companies.

Standard & Poor's publishes a series called *Standard Stock Reports* that covers those stocks listed on the New York Stock Exchange, the American Stock Exchange, and the over-the-counter markets. Information on each stock is summarized on a single sheet, which includes a description of the company, a chart of the company's performance, and detailed statistical data.

Standard & Poor's also publishes a smaller, but still useful, *Stock Guide.* Issued monthly, this handbook offers one line of key data on more than 5,000 common and preferred stocks. Especially useful for seekers of super stocks is the data on price, earnings, and monthly volume. The latter is particularly helpful in determining which stocks are thinly traded (and consequently could be quite volatile).

You can calculate a stock's average daily trading volume by dividing the monthly volume by 20 (the total business days in a typical month). If the result is less than 5,000 shares, be very careful in placing an order to buy or sell that stock. In such a situation, you might want to consider a limited order at a specified price somewhere between the bid and asked prices. A second useful fact listed for all companies in the *Stock Guide* is the number of shares of each stock held by institutions collectively—information helpful in our scorecard calculations. This booklet is available at most libraries and stock brokerage firms.

The *Value Line Investment Survey* summarizes (again, on one page) individual company statistics and prospects. More than 1,500 companies are covered. The listings are available at most libraries or through:

Value Line Investment Survey
Arnold Bernhard & Company, Inc.
711 Third Avenue
New York, N.Y. 10017

BROKERAGE FIRM SOURCES

Much of this specific information also can be found at your local brokerage office. As a matter of fact, stock brokerage firms are superb sources of company and industry information. The larger firms, such as Merrill Lynch and Prudential-Bache, maintain platoons of stock analysts who produce volumes of information, all of it free to clients.

Since you will need a stockbroker to transact market orders anyway, it makes sense to select a broker at a firm that can provide the information you will need on companies as well. Interpreting recommendations made by brokerage firms is an art, and you must learn it before you can use their advice.

The typical stock brokerage house has a research department that provides a steady flow of reports for use by both individual and institutional investors. In addition, these firms subscribe to major investment information sources that also can be used by their customers.

Brokerage houses have their own research staffs of economists and analysts. They make recommendations to buy, hold, or sell securities. Some brokerage houses deal primarily with institutional investors, whereas others, known as "retail" brokerage houses, deal primarily with individuals. Major retail brokerage houses include Merrill Lynch, Pierce, Fenner & Smith (commonly known simply as Merrill Lynch); Dean Witter; Prudential-Bache; Shearson, Lehman, Hutton; Smith Barney; Harris Upham & Co.; and A.G. Edwards, to name a few.

Each brokerage house puts out a number of pamphlets for investors. These reports cover the economy, the stock and bond markets, options, and specific industries and companies. Understanding your broker's language is the key to being able to process the investment information he provides. With dozens of national brokerage houses and hundreds of smaller regional houses—all with research staffs—it's best to know the system *before* you start reviewing brokerage recommendations.

Brokerage reports and comments come in four different types: economic and financial information, investment strategy recommendations, technical commentary and advice, and recommendations on specific stocks or stock groups.

Economic and financial information concerns the national or international economy (interest rates, inflation, the balance of trade, and so on). Investment strategy relates to asset allocation among the different markets into which an investor may place money. Technical analysts try to forecast where stock prices are headed. They might comment on an interesting stock or group of stocks that, according to their price charts, is rising. Technical analysts also follow investor "sentiment," buy-sell volume, and other indicators. Specific stock recommendations are just what they seem to be: advice to buy, sell, or hold individual stocks.

Today a typical strategist would recommend that investors hold only a small amount of cash in their portfolios (i.e. that they be almost fully invested in stocks or bonds). A small cash position would be about 4 percent or what is called "a minimal weighting." For the stock section of your portfolio, they would point to favorite sectors, say, interest-sensitive issues such as bank stocks, insurance stocks, and utilities. Also favored would be some consumer issues such as food companies or supermarket chains.

All of these recommendations would be consistent with the economic scenario of a slowing economy and lower interest rates. The technical analyst, however, might be more cautious (or even contradict the strategist), noting that stock market volume has been increasing when the market goes down and decreasing when the market goes up. This is usually a negative technical reading. The technician may also point out that institutional cash (largely mutual-fund cash positions) is low—another bearish technical indicator. It is not uncommon for technicians to disagree with their own firm's strategists as well as those at rival firms.

Even more confusing is that most stockbrokers use several levels of stock recommendations. Many firms have a five-point scale for rating stocks. On that scale, a 2 is often a "buy," and a 1 is an even stronger buy. But sometimes even a 1 isn't the strongest recommendation. Many firms have a stock-selection committee that picks a "recommended" list from among issues rated 1. Note that 1 is sometimes given to a stock that would usually rate lower simply because the company is an underwriting client of the brokerage firm.

Brokerage firms may recommend stocks from certain industries partly to keep their industry analysts happy. There are also short-term recommendations, long-term recommendations, and "aggressive" or "high-risk" recommendations, to name but a few types. So view any brokerage house advice with caution. While some of it can be useful, always consider its source before following it.

COMPUTER-BASED INVESTMENT INFORMATION

A large and growing amount of computer-based information is available to super stock searchers with computers. Data bases or disks and access to computer data bases are available from a myriad of financial service firms. Among the disk data bases, the best source of financial information for studies of corporate securities and their issuers is Standard & Poor's Compustat Services, Inc. Its financial data base is on several tapes that are regularly updated. The annual tape contains data for 20 years on over 6,000 stocks, and includes virtually every balance sheet and income statement an investor could want, as well as some market data. Quarterly tapes, containing data from 1972 on, are available for about 3,000 companies.

The Center for Research in Security Prices (CRSP) at the University of Chicago produces a set of tapes containing daily stock prices for every NYSE stock, starting in 1926. Daily and monthly readings of market indices are also available.

The CRSP tapes allow researchers to document the price performance of every NYSE stock by itself and in relation to a market index, over almost 60 years. This makes it easy to study the reaction of a stock, or group of stocks, to a particular event or series of events.

Another data base tape is available from Interactive Data Corporation (IDC), which produces a quarterly tape containing daily price and volume information for all NYSE and AMEX securities, as well as some OTC stocks. Quarterly dividends and earnings are also listed on IDC's tapes.

The publishers of *The Media General Financial Weekly* sell a data bank service containing major financial information for close to 3,000 companies. The tapes include current and historical price and volume information, as well as balance sheet and income statement data.

An investor who subscribes to a central investment data base can obtain computer-based information without having to purchase tapes. For example, IDC has a time-sharing computer service company that specializes in providing financial information. By connecting their computer terminals via modem to IDC's computer, clients can access IDC's various services.

IDC offers the Value Line Data Base, which covers the 1,700 companies in *The Value Line Investment Survey* described earlier and can be especially useful for super stock seekers. IDC also provides several programs for processing information such as "Analystics"—a data retrieval and report-generation service that allows users to access data and analyze it. Another program, "Xport," is a portfolio management system that will price portfolio holdings and help the user to measure a given portfolio's performance against several benchmarks, such as market indices.

Finally, a major source of investment information for those with computers is the Dow Jones News/Retrieval Service, produced by the publishers of the *Wall Street Journal.* This service provides up-to-the-minute news and information from Dow Jones, including news from the *Wall Street Journal, Barron's* and the Dow Jones News Service. In addition, super stock searchers can access detailed data on over 6,000 publicly held companies, including data filed with the SEC, plus updates of weekly economic information and forecasts of corporate earnings for 2400 of the most widely followed companies. You can also use this service to retrieve securities prices.

The Dow Jones News/Retrieval is available 22 hours a day. Subscribers access it through the purchase of software and by paying a membership fee. In addition, users must pay different per-minute fees to use the various parts of the service (nonprime-time rates are cheaper than prime-time rates).

The company also offers several software packages that integrate with the Dow Jones News/Retrieval system to perform various tasks such as accounting and controls for portfolio management. Other packages are designed to assist investors in performing fundamental stock market analysis.

Data Resources, Inc., a division of McGraw-Hill, produces software programs that allow investors to access business, economic, and financial information from its data base, which is one of the largest private collections of computerized business data.

Only the tip of the proverbial computer-information iceberg has been mentioned. Personal computer applications are evolving rapidly and coming down in price. If you have a computer, it's worth investigating the software available.

FINANCIAL AND INVESTMENT NEWSLETTERS

There are now more than 1,000 financial newsletters published in the United States that focus on common stocks. Nearly all give, buy, sell, and hold recommendations to subscribers. The investors who can profit most from a newsletter are those who are independent and transact their own trades through a discount broker. If you use a full-service brokerage house, and you trust your broker's research and advice, it may be redundant, as well as confusing, to subscribe to an investment newsletter. But if you're a do-it-yourselfer, or if you just like to contrast opinions, newsletters can be useful. Finding the right newsletter is no easy task. A good starting point is a newsletter about newsletters, the *Hulbert Financial Digest,* which rates the performance of more than 200 sample portfolios featured in 100 newsletters.

Newsletters like *The Chartist* and *The Professional Tape Reader* are strictly technical services that select stocks on the basis of their price and volume patterns. Other newsletters concentrate on balance sheets, earnings, and the economic outlook for different industries. Still others select stocks of a particular type, such as *Growth Stock Outlook,* or even in a specific industry group, such as *High Technology Investments.*

There is very little consistency in which types of letters yield the best returns to investors. Nevertheless, it is possible to select a good newsletter by considering a variety of factors. One that can be used to eliminate choices is cost. Newsletter services can range from $49 a year to $500 a year, and there seems to be no correlation between high prices and high returns! You might decide on what you can afford, and then use cost as a major selection factor.

RECOMMENDED BOOKS

Investors looking for the next super stock can find a terrific selection of books at the local library. If the library doesn't have the book you need, ask for it! Most libraries can obtain volumes for you on very short notice. Learn to use R.R. Bowker's *Books in Print* and the *Books in Print* supplements. The key is simply to know what you are looking for. The community library can be an investor's best friend.

Each year publishers unleash a flood of how-to investment books. Many of them are of the "get-rich-quick" variety and, like some diet books that "guarantee" lightning-quick weight loss, sell on the promise of making you rich overnight. Few of these books can be considered authoritative or worth shelf space in your home. Among those that have passed the test of time (i.e. can be read and reread and still teach you something new) are:

The Intelligent Investor
by Benjamin Graham
Harper & Row (1973)

This classic book teaches the principles of sound investing by advocating a point of view that not all agree with. Nonetheless, it contains rich insights. The late Ben Graham was one of the most respected investment authorities in the past 50 years.

The Battle for Investment Survival
by Gerald M. Loeb
Simon & Schuster (1957)

Gerry Loeb was a successful stockbroker who made millions practicing what he preached: Let the stock market guide your investments. One of his basic tenets was to never, ever average down on a stock, but instead, average up. Most investors do the reverse. Gerry was fond of saying that in the 1940s and 1950s making money in Wall Street was a battle, but by the 1970s he called it a war.

The Battle for Stock Market Profits
by Gerald M. Loeb
Simon & Schuster (1971)

A follow-up on his bestseller *The Battle for Investment Survival.* Worth reading for Loeb's further thoughts.

Investment Policy
"How to Win the Loser's Game"
by Charles D. Ellis
Dow Jones - Irwin (1985)

Charles Ellis is managing partner of Greenwich Associates, a financial consulting firm. In this book he reviews which investment strategies work for successful investments. He goes on to point out that ". . .the overwhelming evidence shows that market timing is not an effective way to increase returns for one dour but compelling reason: on average and over time, it does not work."

Elsewhere in his book, Mr. Ellis refers to an unpublished study of 100 large pension funds. In their experience with market timing, a research team found that while all the funds had engaged in at least some market timing, not one of the funds had improved its rate of return as a result of its efforts at timing. In fact, 89 of the 100 lost as a result of "timing." And their losses averaged a daunting 4.5 percent over that 5-year period! Anecdotes such as these make Ellis's book well worth reading.

How To Buy Stocks
by Louis Engel and Peter Wyckoff
Little, Brown & Co. (1976)

One of the better stock market primers, even though it is dated. It presents all of the basic information in a clear, concise style.

Security Analysis of Stock Trends
by Benjamin Graham
McGraw-Hill (1962)

Somewhat dated, but quite simply the bible of value-oriented investing analysis. It is difficult reading but well worth the effort required.

The Only Other Investment Guide
        You'll Ever Need
by Andrew Tobias
Simon & Schuster

Humor, ridicule, and exaggeration help Mr. Tobias to point out that the hoary maxim still applies to the whole spectrum of "get-rich-quick" deals: There's no such thing as a free lunch! An entertaining book.

Understanding Wall Street
by Jeffrey B. Little & Lucien Rhodes
Liberty House (1988)

This invaluable, easy-to-read guide explains the basics of investing, as well as many of the principles on which *Finding the Next Superstock* is based. Written by two experienced analysts, *Understanding Wall Street* is comprehensive, fully illustrated, and updated at each printing.

How to Make Money in Wall Street
by Louis Rukeyser
Doubleday (1974)

A witty and useful overview of how the stock market works and what makes its investors, analysts, stockbrokers, and portfolio managers tick. Rukeyser's decades of reporting on the financial scene, culminating in his current television program "Wall Street Week," give him a perspective that is both informative and engaging.

Investment Analysis and Portfolio Management
by Cohen, Zinbarg and Zeikel
Richard D. Irwin, Publisher (5th Edition)

An authoritative college textbook on the investment process. It is detailed and somewhat tedious, but close to the last word on the subject and, through recent editions, fairly up-to-date.

Understanding the Economy—For those People Who
Can't Stand Economics
by Alfred L. Malabre, Jr.
Dodd, Mead and Company (1975)

A primer on how our economy works written by a *Wall Street Journal* staffer.

ECONOMIC BACKGROUND

From time to time it is useful in making investment decisions to determine where we are in the business cycle, and attempt to gauge the future economic trend. Forecasting requires searching out and reading indicators that might hint at the future shape of the economy.

Remember, it is the trend that is most important. Your data should encompass at least two key weekly indicators that signal when a trend is about to change. For example, you might look at current figures on paperboard production and railroad carloadings. The rationale for paperboard as a leading indicator is that nearly all products are packaged or wrapped, so a change in paperboard production could signal a boom or a slump. Railroad carloadings figures number the total of all cars being loaded for shipment each week. Since almost everything produced must be shipped, and a lot of shipping is done by railroad, a change in this indicator can be most significant.

Important Economic Indicators

GNP. Gross National Product is the total of all goods and services produced in the U.S. in a given year. The GNP is reported each quarter.

Employment and Unemployment Figures. Percentages are issued on a monthly basis.

Disposable Personal Income. How much money people have to spend after paying off their fixed monthly costs.

Consumer Debt. The total amount consumers currently owe. Too much consumer debt is sometimes a signal of an impending economic downturn.

Cost of Living Index. The inflation rate at the consumer level. (Also called the Consumer Price Index.)

Interest Rates. The prime rate and long-term bond rates should be followed. Pay attention to both the level and direction of movement for these rates. Most Wall Street observers wish they could forecast rates, especially by watching the varied signals of Federal Reserve policy. Unfortunately, few of the experts can predict the future course of rates. Nevertheless, all investors watch the trend—so you should, too.

Commodity Prices. Price changes in sugar, wheat, copper, and other commodities often signal stock price changes in the industries they affect. Gold is unique as a barometer of investor confidence worldwide. Usually, a downward trend in gold means good news for investors, and an uptrend indicates future problems. The dollar's value is also a fairly good indicator of the economy's strength, and a drop in value sometimes spells trouble for major U.S. export industries, such as agriculture.

Economic Data

In the mid-1980s, economy watching became more of an obsession than ever before. Economists and financial experts suddenly focused on three specific sets of economic data to the exclusion of almost everything else. Here is a listing of those three sets of data with an explanation of their importance and some clues as to their interpretation.

1). *The Department of Labor's Monthly Employment Report.* This is released on the first Friday of each month and indicates the number of new jobs created during the reporting period and the number of hours worked as well as other employment-related data. Employment figures show whether the economy is slowing or expanding. A significant low-employment number could signal a coming recession. A higher number reflects that the economy is expanding. That could be good for stocks (and bad for bonds); but if the figures are too high, it might signal a boom atmosphere in which inflation could be a future problem. That would be bad for stocks.

2). *The Department of Commerce's Monthly Report.* This report reflects import and export figures—the so-called balance-of-trade deficit. In the mid-1980s, it became an obsession of economists and financial analysts. The importance of their figures is as follows: bigger trade deficits will push the U.S. dollar lower as foreigners lose confidence in our economy and either shun or sell their dollars. That would force the Federal Reserve to increase interest rates to make dollar-denominated securities more attractive. That would be bad for stocks. Imports would become more expensive and this would result in rising inflation which is also bad for stocks.

In their April 1988 report, the Department of Commerce, for the first time, released seasonally adjusted figures. As a result, the trade deficit-related figures began to lose some of their dramatic "punch" on a monthly basis, allowing investors to focus on longer-term trends.

3). *The Commodity Research Bureau's Index of Futures Prices.* Market watchers believe that this index, one of the chief indicators of inflation, is the most important of all. Daily rises in this index of 21 commodities reflects a heavy emphasis on agricultural commodities and therefore is an early warning indicator of higher food prices *and* higher inflation.

Some economists believe that the CRB index may be losing some of its influence since it does not always reflect overall inflation in the economy. A better index, they believe, is The Journal of Commerce's Sensitive Material Price Index, which includes prices of industrial materials (like oil and rubber) in proportion to their use in the economy. This is a better predictor of long-term inflation. Given the differing views, I urge you to watch both indexes but give more weight to the Sensitive Material Price Index.

Overall these three economic indicators can be helpful in reading the economic data for some ideas of the future trend of the economy on a longer-term basis. When used as a source for a short-term forecast, all three can give false and misleading signals.

A Few Definitions

In reading and developing a feel for the economic environment, you'll encounter terms that have particular meanings in economics. Dictionary definitions won't quite do. Here are eight economic definitions to help you on your way. (See Appendix I for additional investment terms.)

1). **Business Cycle:** The sequence of expansion and contraction in an economy. Business cycles vary in length from 1 year to a decade. Historically, recessions have lasted 1½ to two years. Fifty-year business cycles are also charted by forecasters.

2). **Deflation:** Occurs when price levels are falling and the dollar gains in value and has greater buying power.

3). **Depression:** Usually this word means a deep, severe recession. However, economists disagree on a workable definition, and this discord illustrates the general difficulty of quantifying economic concepts. For example, the term "depression" is often used to mean the Great Depression of the 1930's. More appropriately, several economists have used numerical levels to distinguish a depression from a recession—over 10% unemployment is a minimum for a depression, but the more indicative figure appears to be 15%. In the 1930s, unemployment hit an estimated 25% of the work force.

4). **Disinflation:** A slowdown in the rate of inflation.

5). **Inflation:** Occurs when price levels are rising and the dollar shrinks in value and buys fewer goods.

6). **Recession:** A contraction in business production. Usually identified as two consecutive quarters with a negative Gross National Product (no growth).

7). **Recovery:** The phase in an economic cycle when business begins to improve, and sales and employment figures go up.

8). **Trough:** The bottom of an ordinary, short-term business cycle. At this point, coincident indicators such as Gross National Product and Industrial Production stop falling.

The scorecard section in Chapter 5 lists the financial factor of return on stockholders' equity (ROE) as one of the significant categories of consideration in selecting a super stock. In order to assist you

ROE FOR SELECTED INDUSTRIES IN 1987
(FIVE-YEAR COMPOSITE AVERAGE, 1983-1987)

Industry	Return on Equity %	Industry	Return on Equity %
Advertising	18%	Drugs	24%
Aerospace	17	Electrical Equip.	16
Air Transport	12	Electronics-Design	14
Appliance-Video	18	Foods	21
Automotive-Car	23	Info Processing/Minicomputers	12
Automotive-Parts	16	Lodging	18
Automotive-Tire	15	Media-Broadcasting	17
Automotive-Truck	13	Media-Publishing	22
Banks	16	Merchandising	26
Beverages-Brewers	20	Metals-Non Ferrous	9
Beverages-Distillers	18	Oil-Integrated Domestic	12
Beverages-Soft Drinks	23	Oil Services	10
Building Materials	16	Paper Products	13
Bldg. Materials-Retail	15	Real Estate-Eqt. Trst.	17
Chemicals-Major	12	Restaurants	19
Chemicals-Specialty	16	Telecommunications	13
Conglomerates	14	Textile-Apparel	29
Containers-Metals	15	Tobacco	23
Cosmetics	23	Utilities-Electric	14

in your analysis and to give you some idea of the range of ROE's among companies, the following review of ROE for major industries is listed below. The rate of return is calculated on average equity using income before extraordinary items and discontinued operations.

The Appendices

The purpose of this book has been to develop a method for selecting profitable stocks. Nearly two hundred pages of the text do just that.

Nevertheless, there are investment techniques, rules, maxims, and definitions of financial terms that don't fit neatly into the structure of the book. Such information is here in the Appendices in the forms of statistical arrays and short essays that should be helpful to you in forming investment strategies. The Appendices appear as follows:

Appendix A
Long-term Record of Inflation

Appendix B
Dow Jones Industrial Average—Earnings and P/E Ratio

Appendix C
"Niche" Investing

Appendix D
The 80/20 Rule

Appendix A

Thirty-Five Years of Inflation Trends
Consumer Price Index
Annual Changes in Percent

Year	Change	Year	Change
1987	+4.4	1975	+7.0
1986	+1.1	1974	+12.2
1985	+3.8	1973	+8.8
1984	+3.9	1972	+3.4
1983	+3.8	1971	+3.4
1982	+3.8	1970	+5.5
1981	+8.9	1969	+6.1
1980	+12.4	1968	+4.7
1979	+13.2	1967	+3.0
1978	+9.0	1966	+3.4
1977	+6.8	1965	+1.9
1976	+4.8	1964	+1.2

1963	+1.6	1957	+3.0
1962	+1.2	1956	+2.9
1961	+0.7	1955	+0.4
1960	+1.6	1954	(0.5)
1959	+1.5	1953	+0.6
1958	+1.8		

( ) denotes decrease

Sources: Statistical Abstract of the U.S. and Economic Indicators issued by the Joint Economic Committee, Author estimate.

Appendix B

Dow Jones Industrial Average
Earnings and P/E Ratios

Year	FPS	Year End P/E
1988 (1st quarter)	$144.45	13.8
1987	133.05	14.6
1986	115.59	16.4
1985	96.11	16.1
1984	113.58	10.7
1983	72.45	17.4
1982	9.15	114.4
1981	113.71	7.7
1980	121.86	7.9
1979	124.46	6.7
1978	112.79	7.1
1977	89.10	9.3
1976	96.72	10.4

Year	FPS	Year End P/E
1975	75.66	10.1
1974	99.04	7.4
1973	86.17	10.7
1972	67.11	14.3
1971	55.09	15.9
1970	51.01	14.5
1969	57.02	15.3
1968	57.89	15.7
1967	53.87	16.1
1966	57.68	15.1
1965	53.67	16.9
1964	46.43	17.9
1963	41.21	17.2
1962	36.43	17.3
1961	31.91	21.1
1960	32.21	19.5
1959	34.31	18.3
1958	27.95	18.3
1957	36.08	13.0
1956	33.34	14.8
1955	35.78	12.3
1954	28.18	12.2
1953	27.23	10.1
1952	24.78	11.1
1951	26.59	9.7
1950	30.70	7.1
1949	23.54	7.7
1948	23.07	7.8
1947	18.80	9.3
1946	13.63	13.8
1945	10.56	16.4
1944	10.07	14.2
1943	9.74	13.6
1942	9.22	11.6
1941	11.64	10.3

*P/Es for 1941 through 1975 reflect the average of the high and low for the year.

Appendix C
Niche Investing

"Niche investing"—buying the stocks of companies that focus on a specialized market—is one of the surest roads to stock market success. No two niche companies are alike, but we'll define a niche company as one that controls a segment of a particular market in a very profitable way through its competitive ability in production, product technology, or marketing.

Finding such companies is not always easy. Generally, you must look for opportunities among the small-to-medium-sized companies that not only "control" their business destiny but that also possess the potential for 15- to 20-percent earnings growth over the next 3 to 4 years. The best candidates will offer a return on stockholders' equity higher than the industry average, possess a strong balance sheet (or at least have more equity than debt), and reflect significant management ownership in terms of stock (not just stock options).

In addition, look for consumer stocks rather than technology issues, since the rapid change and short life span of technology products could cause the "niche" to quickly become obsolete. Both the investing public and security analysts find consumer products easier to understand than the more esoteric concepts behind many high-tech products.

Once you've identified a "niche" company as an appropriate portfolio candidate, you must then ask the question: "When should I buy?" Traditional buying rules usually rely on price/earnings ratios to help when a stock is cheap or dear. A better, more dynamic approach is to use the stock's value ratio, which you determine by dividing the stock's projected earnings growth rate for the forthcoming year by its current price/earnings ratio. For example, if your prospective niche company is expected to grow at 20 percent a year and it is currently trading at 10 times earnings, its value ratio is 2 (the higher the number, the better the value). This means that the stock is selling at half of its growth rate, a very attractive ratio that would make the company an immediate buy. Note that estimated earnings growth rates are used instead of past-earnings growth rates. Thus, the value ratio reflects the fact that growth is attractive only if the price of the stock is also attractive.

Appendix D
Using the 80/20 Rule to Build
a Successful Super Stock Portfolio

One of the handiest guidelines for decision making in business and finance is the so called 80/20 rule. Simply stated, the rule says that if a group of items are arrayed in terms of value, 80 percent of the total value usually comes from the top 20 percent of the items. In retailing, typically 80 percent of a store's profit is derived from the sale of only 20 percent of its inventory; for charities, 80 percent of the donations are derived from 20 percent of the contributors; and so on. This rule also works in successful investment portfolios—80 percent of the profits come from 20 percent of the stocks. The problem is in figuring out which stocks are going to make up that ultra profitable 20 percent!

With the 80/20 rule in mind, most shrew investors don't "bet the farm" on just a few stocks, no matter how attractive they seem. Putting all of the eggs into one basket and watching the basket might have worked well for legendary investor Bernard Baruch or fabled stocktrader Gerald Loeb, but most of us are better served by diversification. It's the best way to ensure that the 20 percent of stocks that are big winners will be somewhere in your portfolio.

John Wagstaff-Callahan, a trustee at Batterymarch Financial Management (a multibillion-dollar asset manager), maintains that investors should "spread their risk" by owning at least 50 stocks. While 50 might seem too many companies for one individual to follow properly, Callahan does add that, ideally, these 50 companies should be based in your own region so that you can follow them more easily. Another distinguished money manager, Gary N. Yalen, the chief investment officer for Irving Trust, believes that 10 stocks should be enough, although that number might seem insufficient to ensure adequate diversification.

In my view, the 80/20 rule fits coordinates neatly with another maxim: the 5 percent rule. An easy and surprisingly effective way of maintaining diversification in your portfolio, this rule specifies that you should never have more than 5 percent of your assets in any one stock. The maxim, first mentioned in the classic book *The Intelligent Investor* by Benjamin Graham, requires that you own at least 20 stocks in order to be fully invested. My personal preference is slightly more diversification so I suggest owning 25 stocks at any given time, or, put another way, 4 percent positions in each of your portfolio's stocks.

Appendix E

How Am I Doing?

There are three simple yet essential steps to successful investing. First, you must determine your objective, deciding how much you'd like to make, and by when. Then, you must develop a plan to meet your objective and acquire the skills necessary to implement your plan. Finally, you must constantly monitor your investments, checking your progress toward the target you've set.

The following paragraphs offer some help in getting started on this. Your objective should be a highly personal and subjective target that reflects the amount of money you have to invest (both now and in the future) and what risks you are willing to take. Risk is an especially personal factor, which takes into account your emotional makeup, as well as your available funds. Can you stand to see your stock move down 15 percent to 20 percent in a few weeks (or even in one day, as in the market crash of October 19, 1987)? Can you keep your head in a euphoric period during which your stock moves up sharply? Can you handle a 100-percent rise in your stock's value? Only you can answer these questions—and you must answer them honestly. For help in gauging your "risk profile," complete the risk attitude quiz in Appendix F.

Developing the skills needed to achieve your investment objective is what this book has concentrated on. The nuts and bolts of a well-tested and highly successful stock strategy have been detailed in more than 150 pages of text. Hopefully, you will be able to use this strategy time and again to put together a super stock portfolio.

The final step—monitoring your progress—is quite simple, despite the ponderous connotation of the term "monitoring." Monitoring just means checking to see how you're doing, relative to one or more of the basic standards of the stock market. Unfortunately, there are a number of stock market measurement standards—six indexes and one special measurement, to be exact. Only a few of these standards of investment performance are appropriate to "super stock" monitoring, but you should know something about each of these market indexes, simply because other investors watch them carefully. The seven basic market standards are:

- Dow Jones Industrial Average

- Standard & Poor's 500

- New York Stock Exchange Composite

- Value Line Composite

- Wilshire 5000

- NASDAQ Composite

- T. Rowe Price New Horizons Fund

The Dow Jones Industrial Average (sometimes called "The Dow Thirty" or just "The Dow") is the most venerable, oldest, and most frequently quoted index. In a real sense, most of the world watches it as the market indicator. But measuring your performance against the Dow may be inappropriate unless you are a buyer or holder of blue-chip stocks such as IBM or Xerox. The Dow excludes small- and medium-sized companies, the kinds of companies we're looking at as potential super stocks.

In addition, the Dow is what is called a *price-weighted average,* which means that a given percentage change in a higher-priced stock has a greater impact on the Dow than the same percentage movement in a lower-priced stock, regardless of the stocks' market capitalizations. So, if a company with a relatively small capitalization happened to have a high-priced stock and that stock jumped, say, 10 percent, that leap could move the Dow more than a larger rise in a much bigger company, which just happened to have a relatively low-priced stock. That doesn't make for good statistical sense.

The S&P 500, on the other hand, is a market-value or market-capitalization index. Market value is the number of common shares of a company's stock outstanding, multiplied by the price per share. Thus, in the S&P 500, stocks influence the index according to their market value. So, unlike in a price-weighted index, a percentage move in a large-capitalization stock will have a greater impact on the index than the same change in a smaller-capitalization stock, even if the share price of the smaller stock is higher than that of the larger stock.

The New York Stock Exchange Composite contains all of the stocks listed on the Exchange and is weighted according to market values. Like the S&P 500, the Composit Index's price movements are more heavily influenced by larger-capitalization companies than smaller ones.

The Value Line Composite, with 1650 issues, contains large, medium, and small companies. Every company covered by the Value Line Investment Survey is included. All companies are weighted equally; therefore, a given percentage change in a small company's stock has an equivalent effect on the composite as the same percentage change in a larger company's stock. Accordingly, this index quickly reflects any change in the value of smaller company stocks as a whole.

The Wilshire 5000 Equity Index (compiled by Wilshire Associates of Santa Monica, California) reflects the prices of *all* stocks for which daily quotations are available. Weighted by market value, it is the most comprehensive market index on Wall Street.

The NASDAQ-OTC Composite is a market-weighted index of 3,700 stocks traded over-the-counter (adjustments are made for capitalization changes not due to market action). It is an index of predominantly smaller companies. The NASDAQ-OTC Composite's market value is a small fraction (about 13 percent as of 1988) of the total market value of all the companies listed on the New York Stock Exchange.

Finally, there is T. Rowe Price Associates' New Horizon Fund. It is not an index at all but a popular yardstick for measuring the stock performance of smaller growth companies. Its value as a benchmark for smaller companies is enhanced by its long price record, which dates back to the 1960s. The Fund's most useful statistic is its price/earnings ratio, as compared to the S&P 500's P/E ratio. Usually when the Fund is selling at or near the same price/earnings ratio as the S&P 500, it's a sign that the smaller growth stocks are cheap. Only three times in the Fund's history has its P/E ratio fallen to equal the S&P 500's. Each time, it signaled a long and prosperous rally in small growth company stocks.

Appendix F
How To Measure
Your Attitude Toward Risk

We have all heard the old adage: more risk, more return. Put more elegantly, the higher the expected risk of an investment, the better its expected rate of return.

Dictionaries define risk as the possibility of a loss or injury, and, specifically in investments, the possibility of a loss. There are three basic types of risk in investing: market risk, business risk, and purchasing power (or inflation) risk.

Market risk is the risk you assume by just being in the stock market and exposing yourself to all of the changes in business conditions and investment psychology, and the varying crosscurrents of rumor, opinion, fact, panic, and euphoria. The only way to avoid market risk is by staying out of the market. Once you're in—no matter how safe or attractive your stock is—if the market declines, chances are that your stock will go down, too.

Business or company risk is more specific; it comes with the type of stock you buy. The more speculative the stock, the higher the risk. However, unlike market risk, business risk can be minimized by buying a number of attractive companies and thereby spreading the risk over a wider number of stocks. This is called diversification, and it works well when properly developed (see the 80/20 rule in Appendix D).

The last major type of risk is purchasing power or inflation risk. This is the danger that rising prices will erode the purchasing power of your investment gains. For example, say you buy a stock at $10 a share and 2 years later it is selling at $15 a share—that's 50 percent appreciation. However, you also note that inflation as measured by the Consumer Price Index has raised prices by 15 percent over those 2 years. Your "real return" on your investment is 35 percent, as measured by what your dollar can now buy. There's no way to avoid purchasing power risk. You'll just have to try harder!

It's crucial to both your health and your wealth that you are emotionally and financially able to handle risks. One quick way to check is to take this short quiz. The quiz has two parts and will determine first your attitude toward risk, and then your financial capacity to bear it.

HOW TO IDENTIFY YOUR ATTITUDE TOWARD *RISK*:

The following seven questions should be answered "yes", "no" or "not sure".

	Yes	No	Not Sure
1). Do you like to gamble?			
2). Do you perform well under pressure?			
3). Are you relatively immune to excessive worry?			
4). Given a choice, would you rather: a. Buy Stock; or b. Put money in a savings account?			
5). Do you have confidence in most of your own decisions?			
6). Do you prefer to manage your own investments?			
7). Can you control your emotions when investing?			

	Yes	No	Not Sure

1). Do you have sufficient income to maintain your basic life-style?
2). Do you have enough life, health, and casualty insurance?
3). Do you have enough liquid assets to cover expenses for 6 months if you lose your job?
4). Are you free from large financial demands, e.g., a sick mother-in-law, etc.?
5). Can you afford to lose a part of your money in the market?

"Passing" for Part II requires that you answer all five questions affirmatively. If that is the case, then you have the capacity to invest.

If you passed both Part I and Part II, you have both the will and the financial ability to handle the risk of investing.

Appendix G

The Power of
Compound Growth

Albert Einstein, the Nobel Laureate physicist and probably the greatest scientific genius of our century, was once asked what he considered the greatest invention of modern times. Reportedly, he replied, "The power of compound interest!"

He may have been on the right track. The power of compounding numbers is simply astounding! Just 1 dollar invested at 6 percent compound interest becomes $1.79 after 10 years, $3.21 after 20, and $5.74 in 30. Just look at how the subsequent years add up:

In 40 years	$ 10.28
50 years	18.42
60 years	32.99
70 years	59.08
80 years	105.80
90 years	189.46
100 years	339.30

Note how the total jumps from $1.79 in 10 years to $3.21 in 20 years. That's the magic of having all that accumulated money working for you.

Compound interest is defined as the interest paid on both the original investment and the interest it has already earned. It is really simple arithmetic, although as the years increase, compound interest tables are helpful in computing the total. Suppose you start with $10,000 invested at 6% interest. At the end of the first year, that $10,000 has become $10,600 (1.06 × 10,000). After the second year, your total is $11,236 (1.06 × $10,600). At the end of the third year, you'll have $11,910 (1.06 × $11,236), and so on.

Take as an example the sale of Manhattan Island by the Indians to the Dutch colonists for $24. The transaction took place in 1626, and everyone thinks that the Dutch got a bargain. After all, think of the tremendous increase in real estate values since then. Today total Manhattan real estate values are about $27 billion. But if the Indians had invested that $24 in a tax-deferred account at an interest rate of only 6 percent, they would now have more than $35 billion! The power of compound interest is amazing, and so is the power of compound growth.

The Manhattan example presumes that the Indians could have invested and reinvested the money tax-free using a tax-deferred account such as an IRA or a Keogh. But since most investors usually pay taxes on interest, the power of compounding is cut down to size. However, there *is* a way to get compound growth and not pay taxes on it for some time; invest in a super stock growth company in which earnings growth is 15 percent or more per year (that's after tax) and those earnings are plowed back into company operations in order to earn even more money (compound growth) without any tax liability on your part. In time, that compound growth in earnings will be reflected in the marketplace as a higher price per share. Only when you sell the shares will you be taxed.

As I noted in the Preface, the most significant change produced by the Tax Reform Act of 1986 was the elimination of preferential tax rates on capital gains. Now, capital gains are taxed at the same rates as dividends and interest. Most experts believe that current income is worth as much as market appreciation, but that is simply not true. Earnings growth is still worth more for individuals, because the market appreciation caused by a company's earnings growth is not taxed until the investor sells the stock. Compare this with the fact that a part of every dividend check is taken away in taxes.

Put another way, as long as an investor holds a stock, the investor can keep 100 cents of every dollar of market appreciation working for him, while only 67 to 72 cents from each dollar of dividend income is available to be reinvested.

H. Bradlee Perry, head of David L. Babson & Co., Inc., makes an effective case for growth versus income. He looks at three different types of stocks that have the same expected before-tax total return: 12 percent. The first is a high-grade utility company with a 7 percent growth rate in earnings and dividends and a 5 percent current dividend yield. The second is a seasoned growth company, like Eli Lilly, which is able to grow at 10 percent per year and presently provides a 2 percent dividend yield. The third is a younger growth company, such as Tandem Computers, which has been expanding at 15 percent annually and conservatively could be expected to achieve 12 percent growth for some years ahead. The company pays no dividend now and might not for quite some time.

Assuming all net dividends after payment of federal income taxes are reinvested annually, the higher growth/lower yielding stocks quickly show the benefit of having 100 percent of their market appreciation kept at work.

As the following table shows, even after a few years there is a distinct advantage to higher growth and lower initial yield—if the stock has not been sold. Reflecting the power of compounding, the advantage widens as the time lengthens.

CUMULATIVE TOTAL RETURNS
(After 28% Tax on Dividends)

Years	7% Growth 5% Initial Yield	10% Growth 2% Initial Yield	12% Growth 0% Yield
5	63.5%	72.4%	76.3%
10	162.1	195.2	210.7
15	313.9	402.6	447.6

Investing for the long term will continue to be worthwhile, assuming one is able to pick successful growth companies, the "super stocks" of the future. Some say it is more difficult in today's fast-changing and intensely competitive environment to pick such winners. But the task has never been an easy one, and once you've found a good growth company, the longer you can hold onto the shares, the greater your investment return will be.

So the power of compounding *can* work for investors, on a nontaxable basis. Think of the money those Manhattan Indians would have now if they had taken the $24 and bought some shares of Digital Equipment stock!

Figuring the effects of compound earnings growth in order to help make investment decisions no longer requires arithmetical calculations. Most calculators today have built-in formulas for calculating compound interest. There are also hundreds of compound interest charts available in books at your local book store or library.

For quick calculations, here are a couple of handy rules you can use to estimate compound growth:

The Rule of 72 (Doubling). How long does it take $100 to become $200 at various rates of return? For an estimate, divide the rate of return into 72. For example: At 6 percent interest per year, a tax-free investment will double in about 12 years (72 divided by 6 = 12).

The rule of 115 (Tripling). How long does it take $100 to become $300 at various rates of return? Divide the rate of return into 115. An example: At 15 percent per year, a tax-free investment will triple in about 7½ years (115 divided by 15 = 7.6).

Appendix H

The Six Most Frequent
Mistakes Investors Make

This is an overview that hopefully will help you to avoid making some costly mistakes.

1). *Lack of an Overall Investment Plan.* Ask yourself questions like: What do I hope to achieve? How much time do I have to implement my plan? What are my current and future resources?

2). *Lack of Flexibility.* You must adapt as your financial status changes and as the investment world fluctuates.

3). *Too Much Diversification.* Ideally, you should have no more than 25 stocks at any time in your portfolio—30 at the maximum. More diversification than that decreases your chances of success.

4). *Profits Taken Too Soon (or Too Late).* When to sell is an essential question, and selling too soon is as bad as selling too late. If an investment was sound initially, then it probably will continue to appreciate despite temporary setbacks. Consider the market and the company's industry. Patience, not panic, should govern your decision. However, if an investment performs poorly and its value decreases, you are better off cutting your losses quickly, rather than waiting for a turnaround that may never come. Admit you made an error. Many people cling to the hope that the investment will rebound or that they really haven't lost money, until they finally sell.

5). *Ignoring the Time Value of Money.* Understand the power of compounding earnings, as in a fast-growing company that is plowing its profits back into the business for more and more growth. Also realize the negative impact of inflation and always judge growth of returns net of inflation (in other words, with inflation subtracted out).

  To calculate the true value of your investment return, add after-tax dividends to after-tax capital gains, and then subtract inflation.

6). *Unrealistic Expectations.* Don't view the stock market as a way to "get rich quick." Stocks are one effective way of putting money to work to achieve a financial goal. If you are looking for dramatic and immediate returns in the stock market, you're heading for disappointment.

Appendix I

Investment Terminology

Wall Street talks in jargon—buzz words with their own special meanings. Many of the terms might be familiar to you; others, less so. Fortunately, none are very complicated. Even a beginner can pick up the terminology quickly. To help you find your way up and down the "Street" (or through an annual report), I've listed the most useful and common terms for you.

accrued dividends—Dividends that have accumulated but have not yet been paid out to shareholders. Since dividends are dependent upon earnings, they are not a debt of the corporation until directors declare them. With cumulative preferred stock, where the dividend rate is fixed and must be paid before the dividends on common stock, any declared but unpaid dividends are accrued.

accumulation—Purchasing a large portion of a single company's stock over time, so as not to attract attention.

allotment—When demand for a new issue exceeds the number of shares being issued, the underwriter divides the available shares among preferred customers anxious to buy the new issue. The purchaser's portion of the new issue is his allotment.

amortization—Reducing the principal of a long-term loan through regular installment payments which usually include interest.

arbitrage—Buying a security or commodity in one market, while simultaneously selling it in another at a higher price. For example, if French francs are selling for 14 cents on the Paris exchange and 15 cents on the New York foreign exchange, an arbitrager buys francs in Paris and, at the same time, sells them in New York. The profit? One cent per franc minus the cost of executing the transaction.

arrear—An unpaid debt that is overdue.

at the market—To buy or sell immediately at the prevailing price is buying or selling "at the market." Example: An investor tells his broker to sell his Able Corporation common stock at the best price he can get that day. Also called a "market order."

balance of payments—The difference between the money flowing into a country and the money flowing out.

balance of trade—The monetary difference between a country's imports and its exports. The balance of trade is favorable if exports exceed imports, and ominous if imports outweigh exports.

bid and offer—The prices at which a buyer will buy (bid) and a seller will sell (offer) a security or commodity.

Big Board—Nickname for The New York Stock Exchange.

blind pool—Funds pooled by investors, often in a limited partnership, to make one or more unspecified investments. The investors must rely solely upon the manager's ability to select a quality asset. Since a blind pool's manager is not required to disclose what the investment is, it may be possible for him to access confidential deals that are hugely profitable.

blue chip—Common stock in a high-quality company that is usually an industry leader and has a solid track record of favorable performance under varying market and economic conditions. For these reasons, blue chip stocks generally sell at fairly high prices and carry high price-earnings multiples.

Blue Sky Law—A state law that regulates the registration and sale of securities inside its borders.

book value—The net worth of a corporation (total assets minus all liabilities.) To calculate the book value per share of a company, divide the company's net worth by its total number of equity shares outstanding.

call—A contract that gives its holder the right to buy a security at a fixed price within a specific time period.

capital gain or capital loss—Profit or loss taken on the sale of securities or real estate, not including accumulated interest.

capitalization—The total value of securities issued by a corporation. A company's capitalization can include stock, bonds, and debentures.

"cats and dogs"—Speculative, low-grade securities.

day order—A market order given by an investor to his broker to buy or sell a security. A day order is good for one day only.

discount rate—The interest rate charged by the Federal Reserve on loans to member banks. The discount rate influences the amount and cost of credit available to all types of borrowers.

discretionary order—A market order authorizing a broker to buy and sell securities using his own judgment. This strategy increases the risk for investors.

dividend—A portion of earnings paid by a corporation to its shareholders as a return on their investment. Dividends are usually paid in cash, but may also be paid in stock. For preferred stocks, the dividend amount is fixed, but the dividends for common stock holders vary according to earnings.

double taxation—This term refers to the taxation of corporate dividends, which are taxed once at the corporate level as earnings, and again when received by shareholders as dividends. Thus, the dividends are taxed twice.

equity—Stockholder interest in a company, represented by common and preferred stock. Also, if an investor buys stock ''on margin,'' *equity* is the total value of the securities in his margin account minus the debit (loan) balance.

ex-dividend—When corporate directors declare a dividend, it is usually payable to stockholders as of a given date. Holders of the stock *on that specific day* receive the dividend, even if they end up selling their stock before the dividend is actually paid. *After* this date, the stock price is quoted "ex-dividend," meaning not including the dividend.

fiscal year—A corporation's accounting year, which may be different from the calendar year. For example, October 1st through September 30th of the following year is a fiscal year used by some corporations.

growth stocks—Stocks with an anticipated steady increase in gross earnings. They typically pay modest dividends and reinvest the bulk of their earnings into research and development.

hedge—A form of "insurance" used by professional traders to minimize losses resulting from possible price fluctuations. A trader will hold both a long *and* short position in the same security, option, commodity or future, hoping to offset losses with gains.

hypothecation—Pledging negotiable securities as collateral for a loan.

in and out—Buying and then selling a security in a short period of time.

interim certificates—Temporary stock ownership certificates issued to buyers of new issues until formal certificates can be printed and distributed.

interim dividend—A small dividend paid one or more times per year. An interim dividend is usually paid in anticipation of a larger dividend, distributed at the close of the company's fiscal year.

listed securities—Those securities approved for public trading on stock exchange, such as the New York Stock Exchange.

load—A term used by mutual funds and open-end investment companies. It refers to that portion of the investment purchase price kept by the fund sponsor and used to pay the sales commissions and distribution costs of the fund.

locked in—An investor who cannot liquidate a position without unpleasant financial consequences is "locked in." For example, an investor who has earned a substantial capital gain but would incur sizable taxes if he sold his stock may consider himself "locked in" to his investment.

long—To own a security, option, commodity or future in anticipation of a price increase is to be "long" that investment.

margin—Purchasing securities, options, or futures on a leveraged (debt) basis is called buying "on margin." A buyer puts up a percentage of the purchase price as collateral and borrows the balance from his broker. The percentage needed as collateral on a "margin account" varies according to federal regulations and the clients other holdings.

melon—When a company's board of directors "cuts a melon" they aren't having lunch, they are simply declaring a large cash dividend.

nominee—A corporation trustee or individual who holds securities for the benefit of their true (undisclosed) owner.

odd lot—A stock purchase of less than the established trading unit (100 shares). The purchase of 75 shares is an "odd lot" transaction.

option—A contract that gives its owner the right to buy or sell a specific amount of a security at a fixed price within an established time frame.

paper profits/losses—An unrealized gain or loss on a hold investment. The profit or loss becomes real if the investment is sold.

parent company—A company that owns enough stock in another company to be able to control it.

penny stocks—Highly speculative, low-priced stocks, usually selling at under $2.00 per share. Penny stock prices are often quoted in cents rather than points.

preferred stock—Stock with a fixed dividend rate. Dividends are always paid first to preferred stockholders, then to common stockholders. Bondholders, however, have a higher-priority claim on a company's assets than do owners of the firm's preferred stock.

prospectus—A printed document, usually in booklet form, that summarizes the details of a new stock issue or an existing company's expansion plans.

proxy—A stockholder unable to attend a stockholders' meeting may authorize a third party or "proxy" to vote his shares at that meeting. This is done by giving the third party written authority (the written authorization is also called a proxy) to attend and vote the shares. Most companies supply a proxy form for any shareholder unable to attend a stockholder's meeting.

put—An option that gives its holder the right to sell a certain number of shares (usually 100) of a specified stock to the option purchaser within a pre-set time frame.

pyramiding—Using the paper profits on a stock as collateral for purchasing more of the same stock on margin.

registered representative—A licensed securities salesman who works for a brokerage firm. He is authorized to buy and sell stocks for clients of the firm.

Regulation T—The federal regulation that limits the amount of credit brokers can extend to clients wishing to buy securities or commodities on margin. The present limit is 50 percent of the security's market value.

right—A benefit given to a company's stockholders that allows them to buy additional stock or bonds in the company below their current trading prices.

round lot—The trading unit established by an exchange, most often 100 shares. Stocks are usually traded and prices quoted in round lots. Trades of shares in amounts less than a round lot (say, 50 shares) are called odd lots.

scaling—An investor places several orders for the same stock at regular price intervals instead of placing the entire order at one price. In theory, this helps him to buy or sell stock at a more favorable average price.

Settlement Day—For the buyer, the day on which he must pay for securities purchased. For the seller, the day on which he must deliver the securities he has sold.

short covering—Closing out a short position in a security, commodity, future or option, or returning a stock previously borrowed.

short sale—An investor "borrows" a security from his broker, and then sells it believing that its price will drop shortly. If that happens, he can then buy it back, return it to the broker, and keep the profit he made on the sale. An investor must have a margin account in order to "short" a stock.

sleeper—A security thought to be undervalued.

split up—A stock split. The number of existing shares in a company is multiplied by dividing each of the present shares into two or more shares. If a company's stock splits 2-for-1, each shareholder's number of shares is doubled while the price per share is halved, thus keeping the total value of the shares the same.

spread—The difference between the bid and offer price of a security. For example, if investors are offering $10 per share for ABC Homebuilders and sellers are asking $11 per share for it, the spread is $1.

thin market—A market with few offers to buy or sell a security or commodity. A "thin market" in a stock could be caused by a lack of demand or it could occur because a security is concentrated in the hands of just a few owners and is closely held.

treasury stock—Stock issued by a corporation and later repurchased by it. The stock has no voting or dividend rights. Despite the name "treasury," this type of stock has nothing to do with the securities issued by the U.S. Treasury.

underwriter—An underwriter—usually a securities firm—guarantees the sale of a securities issue at a stated price—even if that means it has to purchase part of the issue itself. More commonly, an underwriter buys a company's stock directly, thus guaranteeing the company its capital, and then sells it to the public at a markup.

unlisted securities—Stocks not listed on any official stock exchange. Such securities are listed on "pink sheets" and are traded over-the-counter.

warrant—The right to buy additional shares of a particular stock at price. A warrant is merely a "right to buy" issued by the company; it does not entitle the holder to any dividends and is not backed by the corporation's assets. Warrants may be perpetual or may cover a specific period of time (usually 5-10 years).

working capital—The difference between a corporation's total current assets and its current liabilities.

yield—The current rate of return on a security, which is paid in the form of dividends or interest. The yield is expressed as a percentage of the security's trading price. For example, a stock trading at $10.00 with total annual dividends of 75 cents has a 7.5 percent yield.

Index

TAB BOOKS Inc.
Help Us Help You!

So that we can better fill your reading needs, please take a moment to complete and return this card. We appreciate your comments and suggestions.

1. I am interested in books on the following subjects:

☐ automotive
☐ aviation
☐ business
☐ computer, hobby
☐ computer, professional
☐ engineering (specify): _____
☐ other (specify) _____
☐ other (specify) _____

☐ electronics, hobby
☐ electronics, professional
☐ finance
☐ how to, do-it-yourself

2. I own/use a computer:

☐ IBM _____
☐ Apple _____
☐ Commodore _____
☐ Other (specify) _____

☐ Macintosh _____
☐ ATARI _____
☐ AMIGA _____

3. This card came from TAB book (specify title and/or number):

_____

4. I purchase books:

☐ from general bookstores
☐ from technical bookstores
☐ from college bookstores
☐ other (specify) _____

☐ through the mail
☐ by telephone
☐ by electronic mail

Comments _____

_____

Name _____

Address _____

City _____

State _____ Zip _____